ULTIMATE
NEW JOB

ULTIMATE
NEW JOB

JAMES INNES

KoganPage

LONDON PHILADELPHIA NEW DELHI

First published in Great Britain and the United States in 2012 by Kogan Page Limited

120 Pentonville Road
London N1 9JN
United Kingdom
www.koganpage.com

1518 Walnut Street, Suite 1100
Philadelphia PA 19102
USA

4737/23 Ansari Road
Daryaganj
New Delhi 110002
India

© James Innes, 2012

The right of James Innes to be identified as the author of this work has been asserted by him in accordance with the Copyright, Designs and Patents Act 1988.

ISBN   978 0 7494 6409 7
E-ISBN   978 0 7494 6484 4

British Library Cataloguing-in-Publication Data

A CIP record for this book is available from the British Library.

Typeset by Graphicraft Limited, Hong Kong
Printed and bound in India by Replika Press Pvt Ltd

This book is dedicated to my uncle, Malcolm.
For playing a significant role in teaching me how to write.
For passing on to me a love of English literature,
an appreciation of nature and a knowledge of classical
music. And for failing so dismally in getting me to have
any interest whatsoever in sport!

Half of the author's royalties for this book will go to
Havens Hospices (registered charity number 1022119),
a charity which provides respite breaks, symptom control
and end-of-life care to children not expected to reach
adulthood because of a life-limiting or life-threatening
condition. I encourage my readers to join me in supporting
this important cause. Donations can be made online at:
www.justgiving.com/havens.

CONTENTS

Acknowledgements   xv
Introduction   xvi
How to use this book   xix

PART ONE
A new job   1

1   **Handling the offer**   3
The package   3
Market research   4
The salary question   4
If your prospective employer makes the first move   5
If you are expected to make the first move   5
The next move   5
Bargaining strategies   5
Reaching agreement   6
The worst-case scenario   6
Considering the offer   8
Multiple and counter-offers   8
Get it in writing   8
References   10
Who to choose?   10
How to proceed?   10
Summary   14

2   **Leaving your last job**   15
Why are you leaving?   15
Don't burn your bridges   16
Notice periods   16
Don't delay!   16
Exit interviews   18
Counter-offers   18
Rejecting other offers   18
Summary   20

3   Being prepared   21
Understanding the job   21
Understanding the organisation   22
Broader background research   22
How to use this information   23
Why have you made this change?   23
Learning from the past   24
Summary   24

PART TWO
The first week   25

4   D-Day – your first day   27
Setting off   27
Into the spotlight   28
First impressions count   28
Start new working relationships   29
Smile and the world smiles with you   30
Nerves and anxiety   30
Not putting your foot in it   31
Bon appétit   31
The calm after the storm   32
Time for tea   33
Final impressions count too   33
Summary   34

5   Understanding your purpose   35
What are you doing here?   35
The bigger picture   37
Why does this matter?   37
Summary   38

6   Knowledge is power   39
Key information at your fingertips   39
Corporate language   40
Understanding protocol   40
Getting to know people you may never meet   41
Skeletons in the cupboard   41
Keep learning   41
Summary   42

PART THREE
The people 43

7 Managing your new boss 45
Assist your boss in their decision making 45
Problems have solutions 46
Be aware of your boss's limitations 47
Good bosses hate yes men! 47
Keep your boss in the loop 48
Conversations with your boss 48
Three golden rules 49
Summary 49

8 Finding your place within the team 51
Developing your team relationships 51
Understanding the hierarchy 52
Becoming a better team player 52
Trust and respect 53
Summary 54

9 Handling your subordinates 55
Ten top tips for handling your subordinates 55
Motivational techniques 56
What motivates people? 57
Setting targets 58
Rewards and incentives 58
Training 58
Team-building exercises 58
Positive imagery 59
Delegation 59
Summary 60

10 Networking and socialising 61
Getting ready to network 61
Networking in person 62
Networking online 63
Ten top tips to better networking 63
Using your network 64
Summary 64

PART FOUR
The learning curve   67

11 Planning and organisation   69
'To Do' lists   69
Priorities   70
The difference between important and urgent   70
Maintaining your focus   71
Get yourself straight   71
Achieving your goals   72
Summary   72

12 Time management   74
Procrastination   74
Just say no!   75
Delegation   76
Dealing with the unexpected   77
Multi-tasking   78
Activity logs   78
Clear out the clutter   79
Relax; take it easy   79
Summary   80

13 Communication   81
Body language   81
Negative body language   82
Reading others' body language   82
Tone of voice   83
Eye contact   83
The telephone   83
Videoconferencing and webcams   84
E-mail   84
Summary   86

14 Writing skills   87
Commonly misspelled words   87
Easily confused words   88
Across the pond...   89
Fully capitalised words   90
Typos   91
Freudian slips   91
Punctuation   92
Summary   92

15 Presentations 94
Preparation 94
Nerves 94
Cue cards 96
Eye contact 96
Physical gestures 96
Visual aids 96
Practice makes perfect 97
Q&A 97
Summary 97

16 Meetings 98
Establishing the purpose 98
Selecting the date, time and venue 98
Set the agenda 99
Prepare the venue 99
Opening the meeting 100
Controlling the meeting 100
Follow up 101
Summary 101

17 Remote working 103
The advantages of working from home 104
How to make remote working a success 104
Ten top tips for working from home 105
Overcoming difficulties 105
Business travel 106
Working abroad 107
Summary 108

18 Working abroad 109
Ireland (Éire) 109
France and Belgium 109
Germany, Austria and Switzerland 110
Italy 111
Spain 111
United States of America 112
Canada 112
Australia and New Zealand 113
The Middle East 113
South Africa 113
South America 114
Summary 114

PART FIVE
Coping with problems 117

19 Dealing with difficult people 119
Assertiveness   120
Team player or bully?   121
Coping with bullies   121
Keep calm and believe in yourself   122
Be nice to bullies!   122
Sexual harassment   122
Developing assertiveness   123
Dealing with difficult bosses   124
How assertive are you?   124
Summary   125

20 Handling office politics 127
The harsh reality   127
Dirty tricks campaigns   128
Win–win situations   128
Gossip   129
Summary   130

21 Pressure and stress 131
The difference between pressure and stress   131
Stress in the workplace   131
The causes of pressure and stress   132
The effects of stress   133
Combating stress   134
Work–life balance   135
What's your work–life balance like?   136
Summary   137

22 Coping with change at work 139
The reasons for change   139
What will be the impact?   140
The importance of communication   140
Seize the opportunities   140
How to cope on a personal and daily basis   141
Keep the big picture in view   142
Don't let it get you down   142
Summary   142

23 Imposing change at work   144

The effects of change   144

The successful implementation of change   145

Managing organisational change   146

Change for the sake of it   147

Summary   148

24 Feel like jumping ship?   149

Why are you unhappy?   149

How unhappy are you in your new job?   150

Don't act rashly   150

Jumping ship   151

Summary   152

PART SIX

Onwards and upwards   153

25 Training   155

Identifying training possibilities   155

Professional qualifications   156

Professional memberships   157

Summary   157

26 Performance appraisals   159

The aim of performance appraisals   159

Preparation   160

Setting benchmarks   160

Dealing with negative issues   161

A win–win situation   161

Possible questions   161

Summary   163

27 Time for a pay rise?   164

Requesting a pay rise   164

Timing   164

Tact and diplomacy   165

Proving your value   166

What to ask for   166

Avoiding threats   167

Summary   168

28 Getting promoted 169

Opportunities for promotion 169
The speculative approach 170
Ten top tips to win a promotion 170
Why do you deserve a promotion? 171
The job promotion interview 173
Money, money, money 173
Summary 174

29 Moving on 175

Laying the foundations: getting the basics right 175
The 15 most common CV writing mistakes – and how to avoid them! 176
My five top tips to make your CV stand out 179
CV templates 179
Summary 191

PART SEVEN
My five top tips to survive and thrive in your new job 193

30 Survive and thrive 195

1. Whether you feel confident or not, make sure you look it 195
2. Make an outstanding first impression 195
3. Build successful relationships 196
4. Watch what comes out of your mouth! 196
5. Fill gaps in your knowledge 196
Conclusion 196

Appendix: The 15 most common mistakes – and how to avoid them! 197
Further reading and resources 204
Index 205

ACKNOWLEDGEMENTS

I would like to thank all of my colleagues and clients at The CV Centre, both present and past. Without them it would clearly not have been possible for me to write *Ultimate New Job*. In particular, I would like to thank my Director of UK Operations, Susan Staley, who has closely supported me in the production of this book and also my 'top gun' CV writer, Katy Wilson, who helped me to research a number of the topics this book covers.

Special thanks also go to the team at Kogan Page, in particular Helen Kogan, Matthew Smith, Jon Finch, Julia Swales, Liz Barlow, Kasia Figiel, Shereen Muhyeddeen, Sara Marchington and Kevin Doherty. I couldn't have had better publishers behind me. Assistance in checking and correcting the text was also provided by Don Elkins and Elisabeth Elkins.

I would additionally like to thank Ellen Hallsworth for helping me to develop the original concept for this book.

Finally, I would like to thank my wife, Delphine Innes, for putting up with my writing yet another book! *Je t'aime...*

INTRODUCTION

'Why do some people thrive from the moment they start a new job?'

Because they have planned, prepared and set out to do *precisely that*!
Once you've successfully secured a new job offer, the next stage to focus on is planning and preparing to start that new job.

I successfully coach my clients day in, day out to truly excel in their careers. This enables me to bring you the very best of what I have learned – helping you yourself to excel.

So you've got a new job

Your application has been successful and you have a new job; what next? People often think, 'Well, I'll just turn up and be myself' – which is fine, and you may well survive, but you won't necessarily thrive! You need to plan and prepare for starting your new job since the first days, weeks and months are critical to your future success with your new employer – and these are key opportunities to make an impact. You've got your foot firmly in the door – but you need to get that door wide open!

Why is it so important to plan and prepare?

You may be the perfect candidate for the job and it may be just the job you wanted, but adapting to a new job, new people, new skills (and new problems!) is inevitably not an easy process. The sooner you acknowledge that and take steps to ensure your success, the better.

As I've said, those first days, weeks and months are critical and will determine not only how you progress long term in your new job but also whether you manage to survive the transition at all! Many other factors that are not directly related to your actual ability to do the job are going to come into play.

You've got what it takes; now you need to prove it – and to prove you're a good fit with your future co-workers and employers – and it's so easy to sabotage this valuable opportunity if you're unprepared.

There's so much you can do to improve your odds of success; in *Ultimate New Job*, I'll help to give you that winning edge to outperform your peers.

What can this book do to help you?

I will show you how to develop a winning strategy – planning and preparing for every eventuality and learning how to handle every possible kind of problem from difficult bosses to juggling heavy workloads and coping with office politics.

I'll take you through the key issues and make sure you know how to not only handle the transition but to really make an impact with your new employers and your new co-workers.

And I'll take you beyond the first few days, weeks and months to discuss what you need to do to move onwards and upwards, increasing your pay and winning promotion.

You'll find this book useful whether you are just starting out in your first job, returning to the workplace after a career break or simply looking to take another step up the career ladder. *Ultimate New Job* condenses the same proven methodology I use every day with my clients and contains all the tips and – dare I say it – tricks that you need.

The CV Centre website

I have made a commitment to readers of this book to provide various features to complement the book online at The CV Centre's website: **www.ineedacv.co.uk**. On the website, I also provide you with the opportunity to make contact with me and my team directly. Features include:

- The CV Centre Forum: You can exchange comments and ideas with other readers and also pose specific questions directly to members of The CV Centre team, including myself: **www.ineedacv.co.uk/forum**.

- The CV Centre Blog: A regular column, drawing on specific questions, topics and problems raised in the forum and elaborating on them in detail: **www.ineedacv.co.uk/blog**.

- The CV Centre Tools: Free CV review, job vacancy database, templates download, etc, etc.

Access to all these tools and facilities is free to you a reader of *Ultimate New Job*.

I have also prepared a special offer for you. If you haven't yet got your new job, then I'd like to help make sure you get just the job you want by developing and perfecting your CV and, when you place an order with us, we will throw in our CV Distribution service entirely for free.

With our extensive database of contacts, we can distribute your CV by e-mail to a wide range of quality recruitment agencies and employers matching your requirements. Quite simply, the more people who see your CV, the better your chances of finding the job you want.

Just visit the following page on our website to take advantage of this exclusive offer: **www.ineedacv.co.uk/9780749464097**.

Thank you for choosing *Ultimate New Job*. I have set out to write the most complete and up-to-date guide to starting out in a new job – a definitive guide to not only surviving but also thriving in your new job. I trust you will both enjoy it and find it useful. And I look forward to meeting you on our forum should you have any further questions.

James Innes
Chief Executive
The CV Centre
The UK's leading CV consultancy

How to use this book

There's no doubt about it; this book covers a lot of ground.

However, I appreciate that you may well be starting your new job tomorrow and simply might not have the time to read everything today! I have therefore provided a 'fast track' below by listing the top 15 questions that people ask me when starting a new job. This should help you to quickly and easily resolve the vast majority of the issues that are troubling you.

Once you've found the answers to your questions, before heading off to start your new job do make sure you spare five minutes to read the final section, Part 7: My five top tips to survive and thrive in your new job. If you only have time to read one chapter, this is the chapter I would most like you to read. It encapsulates some of the most important principles that I cover in the book. Make an effort to accommodate all these when starting your new job and you'll immediately be well above average.

I'd also recommend that you take time to have a good look at Chapter 4, which covers that all-important first day.

An apology in advance…

It is totally impossible to write a book of this nature in such a way that all of the content will be perfectly suited to everyone. Some of my readers will be manual workers, some will be office workers, some will be senior executives. Some will work in manufacturing, some in retail, some in the service sectors. Some will work in a team; some won't. Some will have a boss; some will be the boss. Some will need to manage their time; others will have it managed for them.

I've done my best to deliver a book which covers, as much as possible, all the different circumstances my readers might be in and all the different issues they might have to face. But there will inevitably be sections which don't apply to your own circumstances or where the focus is either above or below your level in the hierarchy. I can only apologise for this and hope you'll be kind enough to forgive me. The answer is to take what you need and leave the rest.

The top 15 questions that people ask when starting a new job

Right, if you're short on time and need answers fast then this section is for you.

The chances are you've got at least one – if not more – of the following questions on your mind.

I have compiled this list based on the questions we most frequently get asked at The CV Centre. It contains the top 15 most common questions that people ask when starting a new job – the questions that come up regularly every single day. If you're reading this book then it's more than likely that you will be asking yourself many of the same questions.

Each question is listed alongside details of where in this book you can find the answers you are looking for.

All the answers to these questions and many more can be found within *Ultimate New Job*. And if you have a question to which you can't find the answer then why not visit our online forum: **www.ineedacv.co.uk/forum**.

The top 15 questions

1 What preparations should I be making before starting my new job?

Chapter 3: Being prepared

2 What should I be focusing on during my first day?

Chapter 4: D-Day – your first day

3 How should I deal with my new boss?

Chapter 7: Managing your new boss

4 How should I deal with my new team?

Chapter 8: Finding your place within the team

5 How should I deal with my new subordinates?

Chapter 9: Handling your subordinates

6 How can I best manage my time?

Chapter 12: Time management

7 What do I do when faced with difficult people?

Chapter 19: Dealing with difficult people

8 What do I do about office politics?

Chapter 20: Handling office politics

9 How can I cope better with pressure   Chapter 21: Pressure and stress
and stress?

10 What if I decide I just don't want to   Chapter 24: Feel like jumping ship?
work here?!

11 How do I handle a performance   Chapter 26: Performance appraisals
appraisal?

12 How do I go about getting myself a   Chapter 27: Time for a pay rise?
pay rise?

13 How do I go about getting   Chapter 28: Getting promoted
promoted?

14 What would be your top tips for   Chapter 30: My five top tips to survive
someone starting a new job?   and thrive in your new job

15 What are the most common   Appendix: The 15 most common
mistakes I should be avoiding?   mistakes – and how to avoid them!

PART ONE
A NEW JOB

1
Handling the offer

Congratulations! You've got a job offer on the table!
But there's still work to be done...

Whilst, in many cases, an employer might make you a straightforward offer and you will be able to accept it without question, there will be occasions when you may wish to negotiate the precise details of their offer. If you're unprepared, this can be a tricky stage to handle. However, if you've done your research and thought things through, your end goal is now very much in sight.

The package

In most cases, your salary will be the most important item on your list but you mustn't lose sight of various other factors which together constitute the whole package. Depending on the nature of these 'extras', they could make a relatively low basic salary appear a whole lot more attractive. There could be many factors you need to take into account besides just your salary:

- *Cash*: bonuses, profit share, commission, overtime, staff discounts;

- *Time*: holiday allowance, time off in lieu;

- *Sickness*: sick pay;

- *Car*: company car, car allowance, car insurance;

- *Training*: training opportunities, training allowance;

- *Medical benefits*: private health insurance, dental plan, health club membership;

- *Pension*: pension plans, pension contributions;
- Childcare;
- Share options;
- *Termination*: notice period, 'gardening leave', non-compete clauses.

You should also take into account the effect this job is going to have on your CV. If it's going to help you to develop in ways which will be of significant value to you in your next job (and will therefore boost your next salary package) then you may be prepared to accept a lower offer in order to secure the job – maybe even lower than your current salary.

Market research

The very first step you should take (and should actually have taken long before a formal offer comes your way) is to research the kind of package usually offered for this type of position. To put it another way, you need to establish what your market value is. It is vital for you to have a realistic idea of what you are likely to be worth to the employer – and you should really have this before you even start looking for jobs.

If you're working with a recruitment consultancy then they can normally help you with this. However, there is plenty of information to be gleaned through looking at other job adverts and by researching online.

Once you've established a range for your market value, you need to decide:

- What is the minimum that you would be prepared to accept, assuming the job is suitably attractive?
- What is the maximum you can reasonably expect to achieve without breaking the deal?

Only you can decide what the minimum is that you would be prepared to accept but your research should make it clear what the maximum is that you are likely to achieve.

The salary question

Whilst you will need to be specific as to your requirements, it is important (with a few exceptions, eg sales and other money-driven and largely commission-based roles) to convey the impression that money is not the only deciding factor in your choice of a new job and a new employer. Instead, your emphasis should be on politely, but firmly, conveying that you are aware of your market value and that you feel it is only appropriate that you should be remunerated accordingly.

If your prospective employer makes the first move

In most cases your prospective employer will make the first move and tell you what they are prepared to offer. This has both advantages and disadvantages. The main advantage is that they have shown their hand and you now know how close to (or far from) your own expectations their expectations are. The main disadvantage is that if their offer isn't sufficient then the onus is on you to make the next move.

If you are expected to make the first move

If an employer makes no specific offer but asks you to name your price then they're certainly putting you on the spot.

Your approach should be to try to identify whether or not they at least have a salary range in mind. An employer will normally have established such a range but, if challenged to reveal it, they will probably err on the side of caution – so don't be immediately disappointed if your salary expectations exceed the range quoted.

The next move

Regardless of how the negotiations kick off, you should be aiming to pitch for a salary at the top end of the range – and consequently be prepared to negotiate and reduce that figure as necessary in order to reach a compromise. This is a standard haggling technique. Start high and be prepared to come down.

Bargaining strategies

The most important bargaining strategy at your disposal is to play this employer off against others. Politely point out that you have applications in progress for other roles where the packages offered are more in line with your requirements – and that you would naturally expect this employer to be able to at least match these offers, if not improve upon them. Whether or not you have firm offers from anyone else is, to a degree, beside the point; the point is to reiterate your market value to the employer – and to establish that you expect, entirely reasonably, to receive what you're worth.

If you're unable to adopt this strategy then your next best strategy is to come clean and state the market research you have undertaken, give the employer the salary range you have identified and then make your case as to why you feel the high end of that scale best reflects your worth. If you've reached this stage then you've clearly already made a strong case at interview – and the employer now wants you. This is to your advantage. However, you may still need to make a final pitch to secure the level of salary you desire.

Reaching agreement

Once you've both got your cards on the table, a discussion may follow – and it may take compromises on both your parts in order to finally reach agreement.

There are so many different ways in which this conversation may unfold that it's impossible for me to provide you with a precise winning formula. For a start, you may be negotiating in person or via a recruitment consultant or by telephone or in writing.

TOP TIP

Whatever happens, keep your cool and maintain a professional detachment. Don't let the discussions become at all heated. Demonstrate to the employer that you are willing to work with them to reach a mutually beneficial agreement. The confident manner in which you handle the negotiations may be sufficient grounds alone for the employer to feel you warrant more than their original offer.

The worst-case scenario

There's normally nothing to be lost in attempting to negotiate a higher salary than the employer originally offers. Provided you handle proceedings in a diplomatic fashion, the worst outcome is likely to be that the employer sticks to their guns and refuses to contemplate a higher offer. However, having come this far (recruiting is an expensive process), most employers will usually display at least a little flexibility. If they do refuse to budge then it's up to you to decide whether or not their offer is sufficient or whether you will have to reject it. Be warned that if you do flat-out reject their offer, the chances of their increasing it at this stage will not be high. Avoid playing brinkmanship.

Another possible downside to negotiating is that, feeling they have initially paid 'over the odds' for you, an employer might be rather ungenerous when it comes to reviewing your salary in the future. However, a bird in the hand is definitely worth two in the bush and, if an employer fails to give you the pay rises you deserve, then you can always look elsewhere later.

An example of a letter negotiating a salary package is provided in Figure 1.1.

FIGURE 1.1   Letter negotiating a salary package

Joe Bloggs
1 Anyold Road
ANYWHERE
AN1 1CV
telephone: 01632 960 603 / 07700 900 790
e-mail: joebloggs@example.com

Mr John Hammond
Sales Director
Boozy Direct Limited
Davidson Way
GUILDFORD
AN7 7CV

1 March 2012

Dear Mr Hammond

Senior Sales Manager vacancy – ref ABC123

Thank you very much for your preliminary offer to join your team as Senior Sales Manager.

I enjoyed the discussions we had during my interviews and this position is definitely of particular interest to me.

However, the opportunities I'm currently pursuing generally involve salary packages between £35,000 and £40,000 – and your offer of £35,500 clearly falls at the low end of this spectrum.

Whilst the salary won't necessarily be the deciding factor in my choice, I would like to achieve a position which offers nearer the high end of this scale – a package which I feel best reflects my worth and my market value.

I would therefore respectfully request that you review your initial offer. Whilst I am happy with the other terms of your offer – company car, bonus scheme, etc – I do consider the salary to be on the low side and would appreciate it if you could bring it more into line with other offers I am contemplating.

As you are aware, I am a highly motivated salesman and have, in my current role, delivered a substantial increase in weekly sales levels, from £45,000 to £85,000 – very nearly double. I believe I will be able to make a similar, significant contribution to your company, which will more than warrant a slightly higher initial salary.

I am naturally keen that we should reach a mutually beneficial agreement on this. Please do not hesitate to call me on 07700 900 790 so that we might discuss the matter in greater depth.

Yours sincerely

Joe Bloggs

Considering the offer

Once the employer has made their final offer, you are under no obligation to accept it on the spot. It's entirely acceptable – and definitely recommended – to at least sleep on it. Such a major decision requires careful consideration and most employers will respect you for taking a little time to think it over.

Multiple and counter-offers

Another reason for taking at least 24 hours to consider an offer is that it will give you a chance to use this offer to influence others you may have received. If you've worked hard on your job hunt then it's not unusual to get to a position where you are confronted with multiple offers. Whilst there are obvious risks involved, you can attempt to play them off against each other so as to achieve an even stronger offer.

Bear in mind that it's not just prospective employers who might make you a counter-offer. Your own current employer might well do so. But we'll cover that in the next chapter.

Get it in writing

Once you have reached final agreement, it is absolutely essential to get their offer in writing. This should confirm the precise details of the package being offered. It is vital to have this in hand before you contemplate resigning from your current position. I can't stress enough how important this is. A verbal offer can be withdrawn at any time and you could find yourself in a very difficult position.

It is worth noting that, in the UK as in many other countries, there is no legal requirement for a written contract of employment. A contract is deemed to exist the moment you accept a job offer. However, an employer is still required to give you (normally within two months of your start date) what is known as a 'written statement of employment particulars' detailing certain key terms of your employment.

An example of a letter confirming acceptance of an offer is provided in Figure 1.2.

FIGURE 1.2   Letter confirming acceptance of an offer

Joe Bloggs
1 Anyold Road
ANYWHERE
AN1 1CV
telephone: 01632 960 603 / 07700 900 790
e-mail: joebloggs@example.com

Mr John Hammond
Sales Director
Boozy Direct Limited
Davidson Way
GUILDFORD
AN7 7CV

1 March 2012

Dear Mr Hammond

Senior Sales Manager vacancy – ref ABC123

Thank you very much for your offer to join your team as Senior Sales Manager.

I am delighted to formally confirm my acceptance.

I can further confirm a start date of 1 April 2012 as previously agreed. Please find enclosed my signed contracts of employment.

I enjoyed the discussions we had during my interviews. As I stated, this position is of particular interest to me and I believe I will be able to make a significant contribution to your company. I very much look forward to commencing my new role in due course and thank you again for this opportunity.

Yours sincerely

Joe Bloggs

encs: Contracts of employment

References

Whilst a written offer on the employer's part is normally legally binding, it is common practice for it to be subject to suitable and satisfactory references. Indeed, some employers will withhold making an offer of employment until they have finished obtaining references.

Of course, not all employers will bother with this formality. With people being increasingly worried, for legal reasons, about giving anyone a bad reference, the whole references game can often seem a fairly pointless exercise. And it has of course been known for an individual's current employer to give them a glowing reference just because they are keen for them to leave!

Nevertheless, many employers will still pursue references and, in certain lines of work, they can take the issue of references very seriously indeed.

Who to choose?

Naturally, you need to choose carefully! Your referees' comments could have a significant impact on your future.

Traditionally, you are expected to be able to provide details of at least two referees – usually one 'personal' (often a former teacher or lecturer) and one 'professional' (usually your current or previous employer). However, it is not unheard of for an employer to want to check not only with your current employer but also with your previous employer and maybe even your employer before that. It all depends on how thorough they want to be – and how sensitive a role it is that you are being recruited for.

How to proceed?

Whilst you could just dish out name and contact details on request, it is much better etiquette to actually contact your potential referees before releasing their details.

Generally, it doesn't hurt to start getting in touch with potential referees early. This also gives them a chance to prepare what they will say about you – and gives you a chance to decide if they really are the best choice.

Depending on your relationship with your referee, you may find it is quickest and easiest to just pick up the phone. However, in most cases a brief but courteous letter will be appreciated.

Very occasionally you may be expected to secure a formal written reference yourself but in the vast majority of cases all you need to do is obtain permission to release your referees' contact details to any interested parties. It's then up to your prospective employer to decide how they wish to proceed.

An example of a letter requesting a reference from a previous employer is provided in Figure 1.3.

FIGURE 1.3 Letter requesting a reference from a previous employer

Joe Bloggs
1 Anyold Road
ANYWHERE
AN1 1CV
telephone: 01632 960 603 / 07700 900 790
e-mail: joebloggs@example.com

Mrs Caroline Carey
Sales Director
Drinks Time Limited
Relativity Road
GUILDFORD
AN9 1CV

1 March 2012

Dear Caroline

I do hope you are well and prospering.

I have recently applied for a job with Boozy Direct as a Senior Sales Manager, having been in my current position as Sales Manager for Stationary Stationers for the past couple of years since working with yourself.

My application has progressed well and they have now made me a provisional offer. However, before confirming their offer, Boozy Direct wish to take up references – both personal and professional.

I am therefore writing to ask if you would mind my providing them with your contact details as my previous employer. You are clearly well placed to provide a professional reference.

I look forward to hearing from you and thank you for your time. Please do not hesitate to call me on 07700 900 790 if you would like to discuss this further.

Kind regards

Joe Bloggs

An example of a letter requesting a reference from a current employer is provided in Figure 1.4.

FIGURE 1.4 Letter requesting a reference from a current employer

---

Joe Bloggs
1 Anyold Road
ANYWHERE
AN1 1CV
telephone: 01632 960 603 / 07700 900 790
e-mail: joebloggs@example.com

Mrs Bryone Ingrid
Sales Director
Stationary Stationers Limited
Pencil Lane
GUILDFORD
AN4 6CV

1 March 2012

Dear Bryone

After careful consideration, I have made the decision to explore other offers of employment and have consequently applied for a job with Boozy Direct as a Senior Sales Manager.

However, before confirming their offer, they would like to contact you for a reference. I am therefore writing to ask if you would mind my providing them with your contact details as my current employer.

I would like to state that I am very grateful for the opportunities with which you have presented me during the course of my employment with you and, should I be successful in my application with Boozy Direct, I will of course do my best to help ensure the seamless transfer of my duties and responsibilities before leaving.

I look forward to hearing from you and thank you for your time.

Kind regards

Joe Bloggs

An example of a letter requesting a personal reference is provided in Figure 1.5.

FIGURE 1.5   Letter requesting a personal reference

Joe Bloggs
1 Anyold Road
ANYWHERE
AN1 1CV
telephone: 01632 960 603 / 07700 900 790
e-mail: joebloggs@example.com

Dr Hugh House
Senior Lecturer
The University of Somewhere
Academic Lane
SOMEWHERE
SO1 9ZZ

1 March 2012

Dear Dr House

I do hope you are well and prospering.

Following the completion of my BA (Hons) in Marketing and Advertising, I have applied for a job with Boozy Direct as a Senior Sales Manager.

My application has progressed well and they have now made me a provisional offer. However, before confirming their offer, Boozy Direct wish to take up references – both personal and professional.

I am therefore writing to ask if you would mind my providing them with your contact details. You are clearly well placed to provide a personal reference.

I look forward to hearing from you and thank you for your time. Please do not hesitate to call me on 07700 900 790 if you would like to discuss this further.

Yours sincerely

Joe Bloggs

Summary

- Whilst you may be inclined to accept an offer without question, there will be occasions when you may wish to negotiate the precise details.

- What is the minimum that you would be prepared to accept, assuming the job is suitably attractive?

- What is the maximum you can reasonably expect to achieve without breaking the deal?

- When negotiating, your emphasis should be on politely, but firmly, conveying that you are aware of your value.

- The employer needs to understand that you feel it is only appropriate that you should be remunerated according to your value.

- Aim to pitch for a salary at the top end of the range. Start high and be prepared to come down.

- Demonstrate to the employer that you are willing to work with them to reach a mutually beneficial agreement.

- A verbal offer can be withdrawn at any time, so it is absolutely essential to get their offer in writing.

- Most offers of employment will be subject to your prospective employer being able to obtain satisfactory references.

- Naturally, you need to choose your referees carefully. Their comments could have a significant impact on your future.

- You should always actually contact your potential referees before releasing their details.

2
Leaving your last job

It's perfectly possible that your new job may be your very first job – or that you are currently unemployed. However, many of my readers will have to face the prospect of how to handle their resignation from their current job in order to take up the new one.

There are of course various different ways of approaching the resignation process, some right and some wrong. You might have decided to leave your current employer but it never hurts to leave them with a positive impression of you.

There are only two points you really have to get across when resigning:

1 the fact that you're resigning;

2 your acceptance that you are (probably) bound by a notice period.

Anything else is just a nicety. But it's well worth being as nice as possible about the matter. Harsh words in a letter of resignation could easily come back to haunt you in the future – not least if you ever need a reference from this employer.

Why are you leaving?

They are of course going to be wondering why you're leaving. The important thing is to realise that you're under no obligation to go into any details. In fact, you're under no obligation to give any reason at all. You could simply tell them you've decided the time is right to 'move on to a new challenge'. Whilst they might be curious to know more, discretion will prevent many employers from prying any further.

Don't burn your bridges

Make the effort to thank your employer for the opportunity they have given you and wish them the best for the future. Keep it very simple and businesslike – whilst at the same time avoiding being cold and distant. There is nothing to be gained by burning bridges. You certainly shouldn't make any derogatory or disparaging comments about the organisation – or any other employee of the organisation.

You may find it hard to resist voicing particular concerns. However, whether or not your comments are justified, using your letter of resignation to launch a personal attack or to attempt to score points is highly ill advised. Your intention may simply be to make your employer aware of a particular problem but such a letter can nonetheless end up sounding vindictive – and is unlikely to ever do you any good.

Notice periods

In most jobs you will be bound by a period of notice, stipulated in the terms and conditions of your employment. You should study this document carefully so as to be aware of precisely what this period of notice is.

You should also identify how many leave days you remain entitled to – since these could reduce your notice period.

Whilst you are not under any legal obligation to give more than this statutory period of notice, in certain circumstances you may wish to do so. If this is the case then this should be made clear in your letter – with a statement indicating precisely when it is you wish to leave.

Don't delay!

Resignation letters should generally be sent as soon as possible after you have reached a firm decision to leave. Your decision only becomes legally binding on delivery of your letter of resignation. It should be noted that you don't need to post your letter; e-mail is also legally binding.

An example of a resignation letter is provided in Figure 2.1.

FIGURE 2.1 Resignation letter

Joe Bloggs
1 Anyold Road
ANYWHERE
AN1 1CV
telephone: 01632 960 603 / 07700 900 790
e-mail: joebloggs@example.com

Mr Drummond Chiles
Managing Director
Stationary Stationers Limited
Pencil Lane
GUILDFORD
AN4 6CV

1 March 2012

Dear Drummond

Resignation

In accordance with the terms of my contract of employment, please accept this letter as formal written confirmation of my resignation as Sales Manager with Stationary Stationers.

After careful consideration, I have made the decision to move on to a new challenge, following, of course, completion of my period of notice.

I would like to state that I am very grateful for the opportunities with which you have presented me during the course of my employment with you and I will of course do my utmost to help ensure the seamless transfer of my duties and responsibilities before leaving.

I would like to thank you for your support over the past two years and take this opportunity to wish the company the very best for the future.

Kind regards

Joe Bloggs

Exit interviews

Upon receipt of an employee's resignation, many employers will wish to conduct what is known as an 'exit interview'. During such an interview, they may try to probe your reasons for leaving in greater detail, ostensibly to identify improvements they might be able to make to the working environment or to specific practices and procedures.

 TOP TIP

As with your original letter, keep your comments at an exit interview professional, not personal. Remember that an employer can't force you to disclose your reasons for leaving. Don't let yourself be talked into a corner. Whilst you may have kept your cool in your letter, it can be harder to do so face to face.

Counter-offers

Your employer may try to encourage you to stay with them, so you need to be prepared to face the possibility that they might offer you an improvement to the salary package they currently offer.

You might very well be tempted to accept such an offer, so it is important to remember your specific reasons for wanting to resign in the first place. Was money really your main motivator?

They may even offer you a promotion or a move to a different branch or department. This sort of counter-offer will take more serious thought on your part. How does the new job they are offering compare to the one you are planning to go to?

Whilst I'm not saying you shouldn't give serious consideration to counter-offers – and in some cases accept them – I would say that you should proceed with great caution.

Rejecting other offers

Besides resigning from your current position, it is also very important to politely decline in writing any other job offers you may have received.

This is more than a common courtesy; it is yet another step in building a strong reputation for yourself as a serious and professional individual.

Clearly the organisation you're turning down has invested a lot of time and effort in dealing with you. They're going to expect some sort of reason from you for rejecting their offer – and you're going to have to give them one.

You might have felt your prospective future line manager was cold and distant when you met at interview. You might have felt the salary offer was a joke. You might feel that your future career prospects would be limited within this particular organisation. But is it really going to be to your advantage to tell them any of that? It might make you feel better but it isn't going to do anything to increase your standing in their eyes. You should always be very careful of projecting any negative emotion into a letter.

Bear in mind that you might end up dealing with this same organisation again at some stage. If they've made you an offer then they obviously have a positive impression of you – and you want them to maintain that.

An example of a letter declining an offer is provided in Figure 2.2.

FIGURE 2.2 Letter declining an offer

Joe Bloggs
1 Anyold Road
ANYWHERE
AN1 1CV
telephone: 01632 960 603 / 07700 900 790
e-mail: joebloggs@example.com

Mr Clarence Kavanagh
Sales Director
Munch Munch Limited
Dogsin Road
GUILDFORD
AN3 5CV

1 March 2012

Dear Mr Kavanagh

Sales Manager vacancy – ref XYZ789

Thank you for your letter of 17 February.

I appreciate your having taken the time to interview me. However, I regret that, after very careful reflection, I have decided to pursue an alternative opportunity and will regrettably be forced to decline your offer.

Please do feel free to keep my details on file for future reference. I would be delighted to be informed should any similar vacancies arise in the future.

I enjoyed our discussion at my interview and I wish you and your organisation all the best.

Yours sincerely

Joe Bloggs

Summary

- When resigning, it never hurts to leave your employer with a positive impression of you. It's well worth being as nice as possible about the matter.

- Harsh words in a letter of resignation could easily come back to haunt you in the future.

- You are under no obligation to give an explanation of why you're leaving.

- Make the effort to thank your employer for the opportunity they have given you and wish them the best for the future. Avoid making any derogatory or disparaging comments.

- Study your contract carefully to identify what notice you are required to give, remembering to take into account how many leave days you remain entitled to.

- Your decision only becomes legally binding on delivery of your letter of resignation.

- Proceed with caution if your employer makes a counter-offer, for example a pay rise.

- Besides resigning from your current position, you should also write to politely decline any other job offers you may have received.

3
Being prepared

Preparation is everything. And the key to preventing any 'new job jitters' is to prepare yourself thoroughly.

We fear what we don't know and what we can't control; yet there is so much you can do to plan and prepare for your new job. Success in a new job, particularly at more senior levels of management, is often built on the thinking you undertake and the focus you develop before you even take up the post. Having a clear idea in your mind as to what you intend to achieve in your new job can be invaluable.

In most cases, you will have a notice period to serve out with your current employer and you can use this time to prepare. The better prepared you are, the fewer your reasons to be nervous. The better prepared you are in advance of starting your new job, the better your ultimate chances of success in your new job.

The first item on your list should be to thoroughly understand the job in question. Many people arrive at their first day in a new job with a thin and insufficient understanding of precisely what that new job entails.

Understanding the job

You clearly need to have a thorough understanding of the ins and outs of your new job – and you should have gained a large proportion of this understanding already, both prior to and during the interview stage. The interview stage is an excellent opportunity to ask more probing questions about the role. Interviewers expect candidates to ask questions – and asking intelligent questions about specific aspects of your potential new role will always go down well with an interviewer.

Prior to starting your new job, you should most certainly go over the job advert, description and/or person specification again – and do so thoroughly. Most employers (and recruitment agencies) will have provided you with this sort of written information. Some organisations are kind enough to send out a whole wealth of literature to new and potential recruits, although most of this will relate to the organisation as a whole, not your particular role. But that's also important and useful information for you to take on board.

Understanding the organisation

Just as you need to enhance your knowledge of the job in question, you also need to develop your knowledge of the organisation. Try to find out as much as you can about your prospective employer. The more information you have at your fingertips the better. If you haven't been sent any corporate literature then don't hesitate to ask for it. Your new employers should be more than happy to provide it – and should be immediately impressed by your proactive attitude towards your new role.

The Internet is also an excellent research tool. Most organisations will have websites where you can read all about their background, their structure, their products/ services, etc. Some will even list biographical details of key employees, maintain archives of press releases, provide downloadable financial accounts, etc. In the space of half an hour you should be able to brief yourself thoroughly. You can also read more widely; there may well be news features about the organisation – or even comments from customers!

If your prospective employer has premises which are open to the public – for example, a branch on the High Street – then, if you haven't already done so, it's definitely worth your while taking the time to drop by and have a closer look. If you're going to work for a major retail chain and you haven't even once stepped inside one of their shops then I'm sure you can see how that might be disadvantageous.

Broader background research

Besides researching the organisation itself, you should also try to understand the environment in which it operates. Again, the Internet is a valuable resource. However, specialist trade journals can also yield a wealth of useful information:

- What industry or sector does the organisation operate within?

- How is this industry or sector currently evolving?

- Who are the main players within the industry or sector?

How to use this information

If you've made an effort to research both the organisation and the environment in which it operates then you will immediately have a head start. Feels good, doesn't it?!

So many people starting a new job know little or nothing about the organisation they are now working for. By demonstrating that you have done at least some preliminary research into the organisation, you underline your interest, enthusiasm and motivation.

STATISTIC

Approximately 80 per cent of candidates at interview will have conducted no research whatsoever.

Being properly briefed will also help you to feel much more confident in yourself. Fear of the unknown is a powerful fear. The more you know about your future employer, the less nervous you'll be when you turn up on their doorstep.

It may even be an idea to start meeting key people in the organisation before you even begin officially working in your new role, although this advice is, of course, more applicable to those entering roles in senior management. Everyone's circumstances are different.

Why have you made this change?

It will also be useful to think back and establish clearly and firmly in your mind why you've made this change, why you wanted this new job – and what you want to get out of it. You need to fully understand and appreciate your motivations. Only when you have fully ascertained what your objectives are will you be able to ensure that you achieve them.

Run through in your mind your reasons for wishing to seek a change from your last job and your specific reasons for selecting – and accepting – this new job. Why was it the right decision? How will you benefit from this decision? What steps can you take in your new job to ensure you benefit to the full from the decision? Understand where you're coming from and understand where it is you're headed for.

TOP TIP

Silly as it may sound, try writing yourself a little letter as if you have been in the role for two or three years, describing what others will say about you and your level of success in the role. Or even write a letter describing your ideal first year in your new job. It should give you some surprising insights and ideas.

Learning from the past

Spare some time to think back to when you started your last new job. What did you experience? What did you feel? What was good and what was bad? What mistakes did you make? What did you learn that helped you to subsequently succeed? In what ways did you make a positive impression? Or a negative impression?

We can all learn from the past. By thinking back to your previous experiences when starting a new job, you can aim to focus on what you did that worked – and it'll also help you to avoid repeating what didn't work!

Summary

- The key to preventing any new job jitters is to prepare yourself thoroughly.

- You should most certainly go over the job advert, description and/or person specification again – and do so thoroughly.

- Try to find out as much as you can about your future employer. The more information you have at your fingertips the better.

- Most organisations will have websites where you can read all about their background, their structure, their products/services, etc.

- Specialist trade journals can also yield a wealth of useful information.

- If your prospective employer has premises which are open to the public then it may be worth your while taking the time to drop by and have a closer look.

- By demonstrating that you have done at least some preliminary research into the organisation, you underline your interest, enthusiasm and motivation.

PART TWO
THE FIRST WEEK

4
D-Day – your first day

This is it! There's no turning back now. It's time to bite the bullet!

Your very first day in a new job may not be the most difficult you ever face in that job – but you can be jolly sure that it will be packed full of challenges. And what are you going to do? Well, you're going to rise to those challenges, of course!

In the last chapter, we covered the importance of preparing thoroughly for your new job, understanding why you've made this change – and analysing what it is that you want to get out of your new job. In this chapter, we're going to deal with how to successfully get yourself through that all-important first day.

Setting off

On the morning of your first day, make sure that you allow yourself enough time to get ready (gather your thoughts, go to the lavatory, check your appearance in the mirror, double-check your appearance in the mirror, etc). And make sure you know where you're going!

It may seem obvious, but arriving late on your first day will reflect very badly on you indeed – and it happens all too often. You're most likely going to the same place you went to for your interview but that could easily have been a month or two ago and your memory might be hazy. You need to check precisely where it is that you are expected to go and then make doubly sure that you know exactly how to get there – and on time, preferably early!

Into the spotlight

TOP TIP

You are literally on show from the moment you arrive at your new employer's premises – so try not to look like you've just arrived at the dentist for some root canal treatment!

Your first day is a lot like one big interview. Yes, you've already got the job but people will nonetheless be keeping a very close eye on you until you've settled in a bit. And you may well have an initial trial period to complete before you can really start to feel secure in your new job. There's undeniably a lot at stake but it's definitely no cause for panic.

Depending on the size and type of the organisation, you may have to present yourself to reception on the morning of your first day – or your new boss might be there to greet you personally. If the first person you see is the receptionist then do bear in mind that it's always worth being as charming as possible with receptionists; they can have a surprising amount of influence in an organisation, principally because they know absolutely everyone. When your new boss does turn up, try to look happy to see them and shake hands firmly – but not to the extent that they end up in plaster! Seriously, shake someone's hand too firmly and they might think you're trying just a little bit too hard. And if you deliver a weak handshake people often think that implies a lack of character.

Whether you feel confident or not, make sure you look it. You might feel like you're back to your first day at school – a little lost. But be aware that confident people inspire confidence in others – if you appear confident that you are able to do the job, everyone around you is likely to be more inclined to believe that you can. It's human nature.

Whilst confidence is critical, it is naturally important not to go to the other extreme and appear overconfident or arrogant. That won't go down well at all with your new workmates. Strike a happy balance.

First impressions count

First things first. Before you get close to doing any actual work, the first thing you'll be doing is 'meeting and greeting' – and first impressions are extremely important. Everyone you meet today will be making initial judgements about you – and often on the basis of just a few minutes spent together. Sounds scary? It's not really. It's what you do naturally every day when you meet new people – when you go to a party, for example, or out for dinner with friends of friends. So don't put yourself under too much pressure. But do be conscious of the impression you'll be making on others.

Make a poor first impression and you might not be able to recover from it. How quickly do you sum up someone you've just met? It's probably just a couple of minutes. Make sure that you make a powerful first impression on everyone you meet today. Start your new relationships off on a positive foot. Start as you mean to go on.

TOP TIP

Remember: you never get a second chance to make a first impression!

Start new working relationships

Your relationships with the people with whom you work are immediately going to become the centre of your working life. Building relationships is vital in the workplace. I'll be covering these various relationships in detail in Part 3 of this book and, further, in Chapter 19, Dealing with difficult people, and Chapter 20, Handling office politics. Getting to know the people you'll be working with is one of the most important parts of starting a new job.

But it's too early to get into any great detail just yet; you're only just starting to meet these people.

In these early stages the most important thing to bear in mind is to take the time to meet people and to make the effort to get to know them. First off, you need to ask for and then remember people's names. (Write them down if it helps!) You then need to find out more about them; start building up a mental file on them.

Avoid talking about yourself too much – for many reasons (other people prefer to talk about themselves; what you say could later be used against you by the office gossips and politicians; etc). Be friendly but remain professional. These people are your colleagues, not – yet – your friends.

Keep your ears open. Start building up a picture of the various different characters you'll be dealing with and how they interrelate with each other – listening to what they say and how they behave. You should also note the way that your boss interacts with and manages your colleagues – and the way they react with their peers and their seniors. Start to get an idea of just what kind of person each is, what sort of character they have.

Whether you're shy or not, don't be unapproachable; don't be a loner. Get all your new relationships off to an excellent start. Make sure you maintain your levels of enthusiasm; it can be tiring and emotionally draining being friendly all day!

The little things count too, like saying, 'Good morning!' and asking how people are. It's surprising how important these little everyday interactions can be. Don't neglect them.

Smile and the world smiles with you

I'm not about to suggest you traipse around all day grinning like a lunatic but... never underestimate the importance of smiling!

Smile at someone and the chances are that they will smile back. Try it. It's a built-in reflex that we humans have, enabling us to immediately communicate our friendly and peaceful intentions – even at a distance. It's such an innate behaviour that even if you sit by yourself and smile, you'll actually feel better for it! Again, if you don't believe me then try it!

Start with a big smile for your new boss (without looking too smarmy...) and then keep a small smile lingering around your lips the rest of the day. It will definitely have a positive effect on the perception that others have of you (firmly proved by psychologists) and you will even feel more positive yourself.

Nerves and anxiety

Nerves can often be a useful tool for sharpening up your performance. However, if your nerves take over to the extent that they interfere with your ability to function, then it's clearly a problem.

Nerves are commonly caused by your having lots of negative thoughts rattling around your brain. Try to relax, calm your anxious mind and think positive thoughts. Remember: everyone – and I do mean everyone – gets nervous about their first day in a new job. It's perfectly normal.

Of course, the better prepared you are, the less likely you are to feel panicky – but you'll never completely eliminate nerves. The secret is to channel your nervous energy and use it to your advantage. Take a deep breath, focus, concentrate and don't let nerves spoil your day.

TOP TIP

You will always feel more nervous than you actually look. Bear this in mind and it should help you to calm down.

Not putting your foot in it

Whilst it's obviously very important to come across as open and friendly with the people you meet, do keep your guard up. You don't know anything about these people; you don't know their backgrounds, their opinions, their characters; you don't know their relationships with each other. So watch what comes out of your mouth! Think before you speak. Steer clear of saying anything too personal or anything which could be remotely controversial or which could potentially cause any offence to anyone. Tact is the word. Stick to small talk. It can be all too easy to say something which you might later come to regret. Remember: EBBOM… engage brain before opening mouth!

My wife made the big mistake of casually confiding to a colleague that she thought her new boss was 'a bit of a bulldog'. It took less than 24 hours for that boss to find out that their new nickname was 'The Bulldog'!

STATISTIC

It's not just what you say that can count against you. Surveys show that one of the most common errors a new starter can make is accidentally using someone else's coffee cup! People can be terribly territorial…

Bon appétit

Lunch might just be a quick sandwich at your desk or, if you're a shift worker, lunch might not exist at all. Then again, in many workplaces, staff often get together for lunch – and there's probably even more chance of this happening if it's your first day. There will probably be at least one person keen to take the new boy or girl under their wing. And that's when you really have to watch what you say! Lunchtime is prime time for gossip and office politics (which we'll be talking about more in Chapter 20). Don't be antisocial but do play it carefully.

You could just turn down the invitation to have lunch together because you have to go down the gym or have some shopping to do or just want to get well away from everyone to clear your head! But be very wary of snubbing anyone on your very first day; your first invitation might well turn out to be your last.

Of course, you might not feel much like eating (that's your nerves getting the better of you) but you definitely want to avoid a long afternoon with an empty stomach. Having lunch will:

- boost your energy levels and help you to think straight;
- settle any butterflies in your stomach/acid indigestion;
- stop your stomach from gurgling embarrassingly!

But do watch your table manners!

The calm after the storm

After a busy morning when you were very much the centre of attention, you could well find that the afternoon is a calmer affair. Your new boss will probably have run out of people to introduce you to and things to show to you and will hopefully just leave you in peace to settle in.

Seize the opportunity to start getting your workspace organised – throwing out those half-chewed ballpoints that your predecessor left behind – and start reading through the inevitable pile of paperwork that will have been dumped on you. There may even be some helpful handover notes left by your predecessor in the job.

You'll probably find it a useful exercise to write up some notes covering all that you've had to learn and take on board so far today. For example, if you're anything like me – I have a very poor memory for names and faces – then you might well want to jot down the names of the people you've met, along with brief descriptions. You can also start preparing a list of gaps in your knowledge and questions you'll want answers for.

 TOP TIP

Your brain's probably feeling a little scrambled and it'd be a good idea to 'download' as much information as possible onto paper for future reference.

This should all keep you pretty busy for the duration of the afternoon but you never know – you might even find some time to do some real work! Even if you don't feel you're achieving very much, it's not a great cause of concern; nobody is going to be expecting you to work miracles on your very first day.

Time for tea

It does of course vary from workplace to workplace but, pretty much everywhere I've ever worked, tea and coffee drinking has been an important task! If you're feeling brave then getting up and offering to make or fetch a round of tea or coffee can make a really excellent impression. It might not seem like much but it's a personal gesture which others can hardly fail to appreciate. If in doubt as to how the coffee machine, etc works then don't be afraid to ask a co-worker to show you the ropes. Regardless of whether you're on the bottom rung of the career ladder or at management level, you're showing others that you're one of the team and that you're happy to muck in.

Final impressions count too

So, it's time to go home. You're probably pretty tired by now but in just a few short minutes you'll be out of the building and away. But before you do go, make sure you politely bid everyone goodnight, smile and leave with your head held high. First impressions are important – but so are final impressions.

There's a chance you might get asked to join a colleague or two for an after-work drink. If you've got enough energy left then a drink or two with colleagues might help you to further develop budding new relationships – but you'd probably be wise to limit it to just a couple of drinks! You've had a long, hard day with so much to absorb and assimilate and you're probably not up to capping it off with a long night out.

When you finally get home, it's entirely normal to spend most of the evening thinking back over your first day and, no doubt, pondering on things you could have said or done differently. But don't beat yourself up too much; there's no doubt that you will be more sensitive to any possible slip-ups than anyone else was. Try to get some rest, give yourself a pat on the back – and remember that tomorrow is another day!

Today's been a whirlwind of new experiences and you've probably had little chance to actually do any real work. In the next chapter we'll be looking at how to get to grips with the job you've been hired to do – understanding your purpose and identifying exactly what it is that your new job wants to get out of you.

Summary

- Make sure that you allow yourself enough time to get ready. And make sure you know where you're going!

- You need to check precisely where it is that you are expected to go and then make doubly sure that you know exactly how to get there – and on time, preferably early!

- You are literally on show from the moment you arrive at your new employer's premises – so try not to look like you've just arrived at the dentist for some root canal treatment!

- When your new boss turns up, try to look happy to see them and shake hands firmly – but not to the extent that they end up in plaster!

- Whether you feel confident or not, make sure you look it. Confident people inspire confidence in others.

- Make sure that you make a powerful first impression on everyone you meet today. Start your new relationships off on a positive footing. Start as you mean to go on.

- Your relationships with the people with whom you work are immediately going to become the centre of your working life.

- Make sure you maintain your levels of enthusiasm; it can be tiring and emotionally draining being friendly all day!

- Try to relax, calm your anxious mind and think positive thoughts. Remember: everyone – and I do mean everyone – gets nervous about their first day in a new job.

- Think before you speak. Steer clear of saying anything too personal or anything which could be remotely controversial or which could potentially cause any offence to anyone.

- Before going home, make sure you politely bid everyone goodnight, smile and leave with your head held high. First impressions are important – but so are final impressions.

5
Understanding your purpose

You've successfully navigated your way through your first day – and the second day is inevitably less of a challenge. However, your whole first week in your new job is undoubtedly a trying time.

I could have titled this chapter, 'What your new job wants to get out of you'. You should know by now what you want to get out of your new job; now it's time to make sure you understand what your new job wants to get out of you.

What are you doing here?

The first question to ask yourself is, 'Why am I here?' Through the time you've spent researching your role and from the information you gleaned during the interview process, you should have a pretty good idea of the answer to this question.

However, the reality of a new job is never identical to your preconceptions of what it would be. There can often be a fair amount of 'rose tinting' going on at interviews. And written job descriptions and person specifications are often put together rather hastily and are often out of date. You need to identify how the day-to-day reality of your new role compares to the original specification. You need to put meat on the bones. And you may even find opportunities which were never originally part of your 'official' role.

Carefully assess your original job description and ask yourself the following 10 questions:

1 Are all the duties/responsibilities you were expecting actually still relevant?

2 Which of your duties/responsibilities are now no longer applicable?

3 Which of your duties/responsibilities do you have sole ownership of?

4 Which of your duties/responsibilities do you share ownership of?

5 Which of your duties/responsibilities has someone else now taken ownership of? Who?

6 Is your understanding of each individual duty/responsibility accurate?

7 Is your understanding of each individual duty/responsibility comprehensive?

8 What is the order of importance/priority of your various duties/responsibilities?

9 How regularly do your various duties/responsibilities need to be undertaken?

10 Which of your duties/responsibilities are time dependent, ie have specific deadlines?

The best people to help you answer such questions are those with whom you work on a daily basis – your team members and your boss. Don't be afraid to ask someone to run through things with you, preferably your new boss if possible. It's well worth investing a small amount of time to thoroughly review your job description. They say the first step to dealing with a problem is to understand that you have a problem. Likewise, the first step to being able to effectively and fully undertake your new role is to have a thorough understanding of the precise nature of your new role. Don't just rely on your original job description – it's just a shopping list; you need the full recipe.

Another reason for seizing the initiative early on in fully understanding the intricacies of your new role is to help give you direction and focus. Too many new employees have a poorly defined vision of their role, all blurry around the edges – and this directly impacts on their ability to perform to the best of their ability. You don't want to see your role in VHS; you want it in Blu-ray! You don't want to drift away from your original, intended purpose but, unless you know precisely what that purpose is, then it's inevitable that you will indeed drift off course to one extent or another.

Many organisations will have a carefully planned induction process for new employees – but many won't! Either way, it is entirely reasonable to ask for a brief meeting with your new boss within your first week or two, to discuss such matters.

The bigger picture

It is also vital for you to understand where you and your new role fit into the bigger picture. What exactly is your purpose within your team, within your department and even within the organisation as a whole? It is a common failing of employees to fail to see the bigger picture – and a common failing of senior executives to see only the bigger picture!

You know what your specific job is but how does this relate to the overall aims and objectives of the organisation? What specific contributions is your team expected to make to the organisation? What is the precise function of your department? Make sure you get the answers to these questions. Don't content yourself with just understanding your own role; ensure you understand its context and are able to see it in the perspective of the bigger picture.

Achieving a full understanding of your purpose goes beyond your organisation and extends to your having an understanding of your customers, suppliers and even your organisation's competition. You want to understand the whole environment or 'ecosystem' in which your organisation operates and of which you are a part.

Why does this matter?

You might wonder why you should care about all this. What's it got to do with you? For example, if you have no direct contact with customers then why do you need to know about them? And if you don't work in sales or marketing and you're not a senior executive then why should you be interested in the competition? The answer is very simple – it is only by achieving a full understanding of your organisation and its environment that you can fully understand the decisions made by the management and, indeed, how the decisions which you yourself make relate to something much larger than just your individual role.

I have already talked about the importance of such research – and how to undertake it – in Chapter 3, Being prepared. However, inevitably, you will learn far more in your first week in your new job than you could possibly have learned by yourself prior to starting your new job.

Your original research will stand you in very good stead but you must now check and correct your findings and fill in the various blanks.

Summary

- You should know by now what you want to get out of your new job; now it's time to make sure you understand what your new job wants to get out of you.

- The reality of a new job is never identical to your preconceptions of what it would be.

- You need to identify how the day-to-day reality of your new role compares to your original job description. You need to put meat on the bones.

- Don't be afraid to ask someone to run through things with you, preferably your new boss if possible.

- Don't just rely on your original job description – it's just a shopping list; you need the full recipe.

- Too many new employees have a poorly defined vision of their role and this directly impacts on their ability to perform to the best of their ability.

- It is also vital for you to understand where you and your new role fit into the bigger picture.

- What exactly is your purpose within your team, within your department and even within the organisation as a whole?

- Don't content yourself with just understanding your own role; ensure you understand its context and are able to see it in the perspective of the bigger picture.

6

Knowledge is power

It should be clear from the previous chapters that your top priority in your first few days is to build and develop your knowledge – on multiple different fronts.

We've already identified a wide variety of things you need to know when starting your new job. Knowledge really is all-important. In this chapter, we'll cover a few other little areas of your knowledge that you will wish to develop in your first few days and weeks.

Key information at your fingertips

A new job usually involves taking on board lots of new information and it can all be rather overwhelming. It's entirely understandable that there will be gaps in your knowledge and that you won't know how to do certain things. The best way to overcome this is to simply ask questions. You will avoid needless mistakes.

It's a good idea to keep a notebook with you and take notes as you are shown new aspects of your job. This should help ensure that you don't have to repeatedly ask the same questions, and will help you to keep firmly on top of things.

Review your notes at the end of each day; write them up neatly if you have time, adding in any further ideas or observations that may have come to you since you originally wrote them.

Corporate language

All organisations, large and small, have their own language. The bigger the organisation, the more of it they will have. No, you're not in a foreign country; you're simply in the modern workplace.

There will be words, phrases and acronyms that you've never heard of before – and which nobody who works outside the organisation will ever have heard before either.

At The CV Centre, we have a whole host of terminology which would be alien to someone who has never worked for us. What does the acronym TF mean, for example? If you think you know then send me an e-mail (ultimatenewjob@jamesinnes.com) and, if you're right, I'll send you a prize! But I'll bet you don't know. The point I'm making is that, when you start your new job, you will have all this to contend with and there's only one solution – write it all down as you go along! And, if you see or hear terminology you don't understand then do make sure you ask. As a new starter, your colleagues will obviously make allowances for your not yet being fluent in their corporate language!

Understanding protocol

Another important consideration is understanding the various protocols of your organisation. Every organisation works slightly differently from every other and you need to get to grips with the precise procedures and preferred working methods of your new employer as quickly as possible.

For example, what protocol should you be adopting when you report to your new boss? Do they prefer you to report to them in writing and, if so, by e-mail or in hard copy? Or do they prefer you to report to them individually, face to face or via organised meetings?

When it comes to working on projects together with your colleagues, what is the protocol for keeping members of the team informed and 'in the loop'?

The sooner you get the answers to these questions, the sooner you'll be able to start making the contribution that others expect from you.

TOP TIP

Write a description of the working culture at your previous employer and write a description of your initial impressions of the working culture at your new employer. What are the differences? What are the similarities?

Getting to know people you may never meet

Obviously, your relationships with your boss and with your colleagues are what matter most at work. However, depending on the size of the organisation, there may be people whom you may never meet but nonetheless need to know.

In many large organisations, the chances of your ever actually meeting the 'top brass' are pretty remote but you still need to know that they exist and who they are. You'll feel pretty silly if someone refers to So-and-so and you ask who they are, not knowing that they're the managing director! Organisation websites, intranets and annual reports are usually a valuable source of such information. You should also be able to obtain organisational charts which show the key individuals at the head of the various departments.

It's unlikely anyone will bother to take the time to fill you in on such matters; they're not directly related to your work. But they're important nonetheless and the onus is hence on you to do your homework accordingly.

Skeletons in the cupboard

Before you start your new job, your new employer is very unlikely to have revealed any of the organisation's dark, dirty secrets – but most organisations have them! And it's in your first few weeks that you will start to find them out.

Skeletons in the cupboard can range from organisation-wide issues such as legal and financial problems through to behind-the-scenes wars of attrition between different departments, branches or even individuals. I'm not suggesting you start poking your nose around, trying to find any such issues, but just be aware that they exist and keep your eyes and ears open. As always, the more knowledge you have, the better it'll be for you in the long run.

Keep learning

The areas I've listed above are just a few common examples. Depending on your own particular circumstances, there could be plenty of other areas where you need to develop new knowledge or brush up on existing knowledge in your new job. Write it all down and keep your notes carefully. Knowledge is power!

Summary

- It's a good idea to keep a notebook with you and take notes as you are shown new aspects of your job.

- There will be words, phrases and acronyms that you've never heard of before – and which nobody who works outside the organisation will ever have heard before either.

- If you see or hear terminology you don't understand then do make sure you ask.

- Depending on the size of the organisation, there may be people whom you may never meet but nonetheless need to know about.

- Organisation websites, intranets and annual reports are usually a valuable source of such information.

- You should also be able to obtain organisational charts which show the key individuals at the head of the various departments.

- Before you start your new job, your new employer is very unlikely to have revealed any of the organisation's dark, dirty secrets – but most organisations have them!

- Be aware that they exist and keep your eyes and ears open. As always, the more knowledge you have, the better it'll be for you in the long run.

PART THREE
THE PEOPLE

7
Managing your new boss

It wasn't immediately clear to me when writing this book whether to discuss the challenge of managing your boss first or to discuss the challenge of finding your place within the team. You will generally be spending a lot more time with your team – and these are vital relationships to cultivate. However, I have to talk about your new boss first of all because, quite simply, no other relationship is more important.

Your success in your new job will, to a large degree, be determined by the success of your relationship with your new boss. You should note that, statistically, having problems with their boss is the number-one reason people give for changing jobs! Clearly, this is a relationship you need to get right – and right from the start.

When we think of managing, we normally think about managing our subordinates (covered in Chapter 9, Handling your subordinates) but I'm going to show you various ways in which it is important that you should be managing your boss.

Assist your boss in their decision making

A common complaint people make about their bosses if that they either take too long to reach a decision – or that they fail to reach one at all! Or, even worse, feeling incapable of finding the time to reach an appropriate decision, they simply play it safe and say 'No!'

Decision making is an essential part of your boss's role – and their ability to make appropriate decisions is also very important to your own role.

So, right from the start in your new job, you need to help them to make their decisions – and here are 10 useful ways to help you to achieve just that:

1   Make sure they are fully aware of all the facts they need to be aware of.

2   Express these facts as clearly and concisely as possible, eliminating confusion.

3   Make use of tables, graphics and other visuals to aid their understanding.

4   Foresee – and hence counter – any possible misunderstandings or objections.

5   Avoid referring to previous discussions or correspondence; it's better to repeat yourself.

6   Make it quite clear what the advantages and disadvantages, pros and cons are.

7   Explain what the consequences might be in the absence of an appropriate decision.

8   If appropriate, present them with a variety of well-considered options to choose from.

9   Tell them, plainly and clearly, exactly what kind of decision you are expecting from them.

10   In the absence of a decision, do follow up with them as necessary!

Your boss is most likely a very busy person with multiple demands on their time. (Aren't we all!) Their time is precious and you don't want to waste it.

TOP TIP

Make a list of what you think to be important in developing an effective working relationship with your boss. Ask yourself, if you showed the list to your new boss, whether or not they'd agree with what you've said.

Problems have solutions

Your boss doesn't want problems; they want solutions!

So much of a boss's time is taken up (and often wasted) in dealing with problems. So many people think that, if there's a problem, then it's the boss's job to deal with it. Yes, it may be their ultimate responsibility to deal with it – but it's a shared responsibility. If you're capable of identifying the problem then you must be capable of identifying possible solutions, even if you are new to the job.

Don't just present the problem to your boss and expect them to deal with it. Help them to deal with it. Don't just go to them with problems; go to them with possible solutions too.

Even better, before approaching your boss with a problem, ask yourself whether it really requires their attention. Not every problem needs to be reported back to the boss just for the sake of it. As Ross Perot said, 'If you see a snake, just kill it!' Feel free to tell your boss afterwards – but telling them beforehand will just add to their stress levels and they won't thank you for it. Deal with the problem first and then take the credit for it afterwards!

Be aware of your boss's limitations

In *The Peter Principle*, Laurence J Peter states, 'In a hierarchy every employee tends to rise to his level of incompetence… in time every post tends to be occupied by an employee who is incompetent to carry out its duties…' That's your boss!

(Peter goes on to say, 'Work is accomplished by those employees who have not yet reached their level of incompetence.' Hopefully, that's you!)

Seriously, approaching your relationship with your new boss with the above in mind isn't going to be particularly constructive. The point Laurence J Peter is trying to illustrate is that you shouldn't necessarily expect your boss to be an expert in all that you do. You're the expert at what you do. Your boss's job is to manage you whilst you do it.

Peter also coined the expression 'managing upward', which encapsulates the concept of a subordinate finding ways to subtly 'manage' their superiors so as to limit the damage they might otherwise be capable of causing!

Most bosses are best kept well out of micromanagement. Because of their lack of day-to-day knowledge of the issues in hand, their decisions can often end up being misguided. It is your responsibility to keep your boss informed without bogging them down in unnecessary detail.

Don't baffle your boss with a level of detail that they simply don't need to have. Simplify issues as appropriate.

Good bosses hate yes men!

Be aware that your boss doesn't always want to hear what you might think they want to hear!

If you truly agree with their opinion/decision/policy, then, by all means, do tell them so. But if you don't agree, then don't be afraid to speak up, even if you are new to the organisation. Bosses who are surrounded by yes men are unlikely to get very far. It's not very constructive when nobody ever questions you or draws your attention to issues you might have overlooked. Bosses are fallible – and, unless your boss is Attila the Hun, they should recognise their fallibility and should appreciate constructive feedback.

If you keep your ideas and opinions to yourself or are hesitant about expressing disagreement then you're unlikely to be doing a favour to either yourself or your boss.

Just make sure you express yourself tactfully and diplomatically; bosses often also hate criticism!

Keep your boss in the loop

Help your boss to manage you by keeping them in the loop on your activities – without reporting back to them every single move you make. It should be on a 'need to know' basis!

Your goal here is to reassure your boss that (a) you know what you're doing and (b) everything is consequently under control.

Don't pester them unnecessarily; just keep them informed on a regular basis as to all issues it would help them to know about.

Conversations with your boss

As you start out in your new job, there may well be a number of important issues which you wish to raise and discuss with your boss, for example possible training needs, your plans to implement certain changes in your new workplace, etc. As a new broom, you may just have some bright ideas which you feel you need to put forward. So how to go about this?

Rather than just barging in on your boss and striking up a conversation, it's normally best to forewarn your boss that you'd like a 'quick word' about whatever it is that's on your mind and ask them when would be a convenient time for you to sit down and have a chat. Let them choose when that time would be, because getting your boss at the right time is often half the battle!

Once you've got their full attention then don't waste it. Make sure you've prepared beforehand precisely what it is that you have to say, that you've thought through any possible questions your boss might come back to you with and, essentially, that you have a clear game plan in your mind for how you're going to manage and steer the conversation.

The reason you need to speak to your boss is obviously because some sort of decision is required on their part. You should therefore refer back to my guidelines above on assisting your boss in their decision making. If you want them to reach a positive decision then help them to do so.

You should also be using this personal one-on-one time with your new boss to start building a rapport with them and to start getting a better handle on their expectations of you. Carefully observe how they respond to the case you put before them. Whilst it may only be a quick face-to-face chat, they might reveal a lot about their opinions, beliefs and management style.

Three golden rules

Before concluding this chapter, I'd just like to list three little golden rules for your relationship with your boss. Ignore them at your peril!

1 Never, ever criticise or complain about your boss behind their back.

2 Resist all temptation of insubordination; respect your boss's authority over you.

3 Remember that, if you can make your boss look good, you will also look good.

Summary

- No other working relationship is more important than your relationship with your new boss.

- Statistically, having problems with their boss is the number-one reason people give for changing jobs!

- Decision making is an essential part of your boss's role – so you need to help them to make their decisions.

- Your boss is most likely a very busy person with multiple demands on their time. Their time is precious and you don't want to waste it.

- Your boss doesn't want problems; they want solutions!

- If you're capable of identifying a problem then you must be capable of identifying possible solutions.

- Don't baffle your boss with a level of detail that they simply don't need to have. Simplify issues as appropriate.

- If you keep your ideas and opinions to yourself or are hesitant about expressing disagreement then you're unlikely to be doing a favour to either yourself or your boss.

- Use any face-to-face time with your new boss to start building a rapport with them and to start getting a better handle on their expectations of you.

8

Finding your place within the team

Teamwork is essential in the vast majority of work environments. It requires four core abilities:

1 the ability to communicate effectively with others;

2 the ability to recognise and understand the viewpoints of others;

3 the ability to appreciate the contribution you are expected to make;

4 the ability to build strong interpersonal relationships.

Communication is obviously key – and we'll be covering that in greater detail in Chapter 13. For now, I'm going to focus on developing your team relationships.

Developing your team relationships

There are many working relationships which exist within an organisation, and how effective these relationships are can play a significant role in dictating the overall effectiveness of the organisation.

Good relationships are built on a culture of cooperation where each individual is working towards the achievement of shared aims and objectives.

Before you can set about establishing effective working relationships in your new job, it is important to remember that everyone is unique and, as a result, has differing needs, emotions and objectives. It is impossible to build a relationship with someone unless you have a good understanding of what these things are and are able to accept them. The most effective way of coming to understand your colleagues is to establish effective channels of communication with them and to listen carefully to what they have to say. This should lead to mutual respect and understanding being established and is a key factor in developing a good working relationship. If the relationship is a productive one, people will have no difficulty in being open and honest about their feelings. By making people feel that you respect and value their point of view, more effective relationships can be established.

Working relationships are very important because they can provide you with an ally, someone who can support your cause and who can help you to resolve problems. The relationship has to be a two-way street where you both offer each other advice and support rather than one person doing all the talking and the other expected to do all the listening and advising. It is also important to publicly acknowledge the important role the working relationship plays in any successes that you enjoy together.

TOP TIP

Identify which of your colleagues appear to be particularly successful in their roles. Why are they successful? What do they have in common? What can you do to emulate them?

Understanding the hierarchy

You should also try to get a grip on how different people relate to each other. There may be a formal hierarchy of some sort. However, in just the same way that your real job will differ in various ways from your official job description, you will find that the formal hierarchy and the 'real' hierarchy are somewhat different. Just by looking and listening and quietly and carefully observing, you should soon be able to see who has what degree of power, seniority, etc.

Becoming a better team player

Top team players don't fit into any particular mould but what they have in common is that they really care about what the team is trying to achieve and want to make a positive contribution to its success – without needing to have their arm twisted!

You should always be striving to become a better team player tomorrow than you are today. Here are my top 10 key tips to help you become just that:

1 Actively participate. Fully engage in the work of the team. Resist the temptation of sitting passively on the sidelines. Volunteer to contribute. Pitch in!

2 Remember The Golden Rule: You should treat others as you would like them to treat you – even if you might sometimes feel they deserve otherwise!

3 Treat members of your team as individuals. Recognise and appreciate the uniqueness of their experience, knowledge, opinions and points of view.

4 Don't hold back on sharing your own experience, knowledge, opinions and point of view.

5 Seek to generate creativity and innovation. Promote divergent points of view. Benefit from your differences.

6 Seize the initiative in finding solutions to any problems your team might encounter. People don't want problems; they want solutions.

7 A problem shared is a problem halved. Let your team members know that they can come to you with problems and you'll help them to find solutions.

8 Yes, it's a great cliché of business theory, but remember that there is no 'I' in 'team'! What is in the best interests of the team should generally coincide with your own best interests.

9 Be prepared to 'take one for the team', ie willingly make a personal sacrifice for the benefit of the team. There are few surer ways to get the respect of your colleagues.

10 Accept the mistakes of others with good grace – and don't compound your own mistakes by trying to hide them. We all learn from our mistakes – and from the mistakes of others.

Trust and respect

Trust is a key factor in ensuring the success of any working relationship, as is respect. By demonstrating the ability to keep your colleagues' confidences, you will earn their trust and they will therefore reward you with the same courtesy. The minute there is any suspicion of people working against each other or behind their backs, trust will be lost and it can be impossible to regain. If you disagree strongly with something that a colleague has said or done, it is much better to address this with them directly rather than taking it up with a manager.

A great deal of time and effort should be invested in the development of working relationships to ensure that they are mutually beneficial and productive, especially in the first few weeks in your new job. You should encourage your colleagues to express their feelings and, if possible, interact with them in a relaxed, informal environment as this can help them to feel more comfortable about voicing their opinions. Listen carefully to what they have to say and share your own feelings with them. Making the relationship work both ways will help to encourage mutual trust and respect.

Summary

- Teamwork is essential in the vast majority of work environments.

- Teamwork requires you to communicate effectively with others, recognising and understanding their viewpoints and appreciating the contribution they are expected to make.

- It also requires the ability to build strong interpersonal relationships.

- Good relationships are built on a culture of cooperation where each individual is working towards the achievement of shared aims and objectives.

- It is important to remember that everyone is unique and, as a result, has differing needs, emotions and objectives.

- It is impossible to build a relationship with someone unless you have a good understanding of what these things are and are able to accept them.

- Just by looking and listening you should soon be able to see who has what degree of power, seniority, etc.

- The most effective way of coming to understand your colleagues is to establish effective channels of communication with them and to listen carefully to what they have to say.

- Working relationships are very important because they can provide you with an ally, someone who can support your cause and who can help you to resolve problems.

- By demonstrating the ability to keep your colleague's confidences, you will earn their trust and they will therefore reward you with the same courtesy.

- If you disagree strongly with something that a colleague has said or done, address this with them directly rather than taking it up with a manager.

- A great deal of time and effort should be invested in the development of working relationships to ensure that they are mutually beneficial and productive.

9
Handling your subordinates

I fully accept that the majority of jobs don't involve your having to handle subordinates. But this chapter is for the minority which do, because, for that minority, it's a vital part of their role in their new job.

Albert Einstein said, 'I never teach my pupils; I only attempt to provide the conditions in which they can learn.' Successful people management is a lot like successful teaching – you need to inspire and motivate. That's what really counts. That's your job. Good leaders follow specific plans and put their subordinates first. But they don't make the mistake of trying to be everyone's best friend...

Ten top tips for handling your subordinates

Here are my 10 top tips for effectively handling and managing your subordinates:

1 Do develop good working relationships with your subordinates but be wary of becoming too emotionally close. It can weaken and undermine your authority.

2 Be fair. Treat your subordinates all equally and objectively. Avoid having favourites. And treat them all as you would wish to be treated yourself.

3 Be prepared to put on your cross face and to take appropriate measures with those who fail to perform to the required standards. But use it sparingly!

4   Praise in public; criticise in private. Never humiliate a subordinate. You want them on your side, not working against you.

5   Don't lose your temper and never yell and shout. It just makes you look weak, foolish and out of control.

6   Demonstrate empathy and the ability to understand their own individual points of view. Make them feel understood and their opinions recognised.

7   Do demand the best of people that they can achieve – but be aware of their limitations and don't make excessive demands; it's counterproductive.

8   If a subordinate comes to you for help, give them the time and attention they deserve. It's your job to help them – and to teach them how to help themselves.

9   Remember that you're not God. You don't know it all. A little humility and a little less arrogance will only increase your subordinates' opinion of you.

10   You'll most likely be somebody else's subordinate. Don't hesitate to seek their advice or intervention if you are worried about how to handle a situation.

Motivational techniques

The most successful managers and executives achieve their objectives by aligning the aims of their employees with those of their organisation. Once an employee is able to understand – and empathise with – the overall aims of the organisation, they are normally much more motivated to help achieve them. Having ensured that the organisation and your subordinates are working towards the same objectives, you can then focus on exactly which motivational techniques can be implemented to facilitate the achievement of these goals. A well-motivated workforce is a more productive workforce. It is also one which tends to experience lower stress levels, lower absenteeism and increased job satisfaction and self-confidence.

It is clear that there are both positive and negative motivational factors which can lead to the achievement of objectives – and these can be summarised as either 'fear' or 'reward' factors. Some managers tend to believe that by shouting, swearing or otherwise intimidating and threatening their employees, they can drive them forward to the achievement of their targets and objectives. This fear factor can indeed lead to good results in the short term, but in the long term the employees are likely to be more focused upon whether or not they will be keeping their jobs than upon fulfilling overall business objectives – and they're unlikely to be very happy. Similarly, being an exacting taskmaster and setting overly ambitious targets can also have a negative impact on employee motivation – since there is only so much effort an individual is likely to put into their job when they feel neither valued nor rewarded as a result of their hard work.

Positive motivational factors are many and varied and, although these may lead to long-term gains, they too can have negative aspects to them. Offering rewards and incentives is indeed motivational but it is important to make sure that these are deserved and that recognition is given to the right person at the right time. Also, although some healthy competition is advantageous, it is not necessarily advisable to use rewards to encourage employees to work against each other. They should be working together. Schemes which prompt individuals to act primarily in their own best interests are normally to the detriment of the organisation as a whole.

What motivates people?

The first step towards achieving and maintaining a motivated workforce lies in understanding the differing factors which motivate individuals within a team – something regarded as an inspiring force to one team member may be anathema to another. There are many ways of determining the motivations of your employees but probably the most successful way is simply to ask them! Although this may sound relatively obvious, by actually showing your employees you are sincerely interested in finding out what drives them, you are taking the first step towards motivating them. All employees like to feel valued and appreciated, so knowing that their managers are concerned with making possible changes to their advantage will encourage them to be forthcoming with their feedback.

You can ascertain the opinions of the workforce either by holding one-on-one meetings with members of the team or by asking them to complete feedback forms or questionnaires. Both techniques have obvious advantages and disadvantages but, whatever system you employ, you need to establish how your subordinates perceive the overall objectives of the organisation and exactly which processes or procedures used within the organisation motivate them – or demotivate them. You should try to identify forces which they consider to be their personal motivators both at home and at work.

It is also important to understand whether or not they feel valued by the organisation in the same way as the organisation values its customers. If this is not the case, then their motivation levels may decrease as, once again, they feel undervalued. If they raise any particular concerns or issues such as overly long working hours or a lack of definable objectives, take care to address these; otherwise the team may begin to feel that the whole exercise has been fruitless. 'Management' often has a reputation – and often justly deserved – for launching such initiatives and then only paying lip service to the results.

Having successfully identified exactly what motivates your staff, you then need to decide how best to go about setting up a motivational working environment.

Setting targets

Most people do tend to perform better when they have a target to work towards. This helps to drive them forward and keep them motivated and, if they achieve it, can significantly increase their self-confidence. However, it is essential that targets are not only challenging but also realistic. It's a fine balance. Someone who works as hard as they can to reach a target that is looking increasingly unattainable will eventually become demotivated and can end up underperforming, making the targets counterproductive.

Rewards and incentives

Rewards do not necessarily have to be financial for them to be motivational. As already discussed, different people respond in different ways to the various incentives that an organisation can offer. Whilst some people are driven by the desire to earn more cash, to be awarded a company car, etc, others may respond more favourably to the prospect of promotion or simply additional responsibility. Or they may prefer to receive formal recognition for their personal achievements. It is important to recognise the successes of your staff; by your showing them that they are valued, their confidence will improve and they will be more likely to reward you with their commitment in the future.

It is also important to remember that what motivates you may very well be different from that which motivates your workforce. You need to be able to walk in other people's shoes. Nobody said being the boss was easy!

Training

Proper training and coaching can also lead to your workforce becoming more motivated. By your clearly showing them how to break down challenges into easily achievable tasks using both instruction and demonstration, your staff should feel less daunted by future tasks and projects, more able to cope and, therefore, more motivated. This form of training can take place either in the workplace or outside it, for example combined with a team-building exercise.

Team-building exercises

People's responses to team-building exercises are generally mixed. Some may feel uncomfortable being placed in what they may see as a competitive environment, whereas others will thrive. However, team-building exercises do have significant advantages in terms of encouraging people to work together in an environment outside the office. They also present the opportunity for individuals to be part of a winning team, within a challenging situation, where each team member is placed on an equal footing from the outset. Strengthened relationships within a team can improve productivity, morale and motivation and result in a generally happier working environment. People are also encouraged to learn from each other in team-building exercises and the competition within a non-work environment is generally considered to be healthy. Activities outside the office can also help people to relax and overcome any contentious issues or divisions that may have been causing problems.

The key to successful team-building exercises is to ensure they are designed in such a way as to recognise the individual strengths and weaknesses of all the delegates; otherwise the competition may appear unbalanced. It is useful to encourage people to express their creativity whilst also enabling them to use their initiative and take the lead when required.

The time and effort you invest in ensuring your team is successful will reap benefits when team members begin to demonstrate increased levels of productivity and an ability to resolve complex issues without your direct involvement. Encouragement towards autonomous decision making and additional responsibility will also help to make sure the team remains motivated by reassuring members of the value of the contribution they are individually making.

Positive imagery

Motivational posters may be a corporate cliché – but, whilst they might sometimes seem a little silly, they do in fact work and so you should seriously consider using them. Office walls and noticeboards are ideal places to post signs with a motivational theme or message. This can take the form of slogans or quotes from inspirational celebrities or professionals, or even positive pictures and images. If your staff are able to visualise potential success and achievement in themselves, this will inevitably help to inspire them.

Delegation

Another important aspect of handling your subordinates is delegation – but we'll be covering this in detail in Chapter 12, Time management.

Summary

- Successful people management is a lot like successful teaching – you need to inspire and motivate. That's what really counts. That's your job.

- Good leaders follow specific plans and put their subordinates first.

- The most successful managers and executives achieve their objectives by aligning the aims of their employees with those of their organisation.

- A well-motivated workforce is more productive, experiences lower stress levels, lower absenteeism and increased job satisfaction and self-confidence.

- Offering rewards and incentives is motivational but it is important to make sure that these are deserved and that recognition is given to the right person at the right time.

- There are many ways of determining the motivations of your employees but probably the most successful way is simply to ask them!

- You can ascertain the opinions of the workforce either by holding one-on-one meetings with members of the team or by asking them to complete feedback forms or questionnaires.

- It is essential that any targets you set are not only challenging but also realistic. It's a fine balance.

- Rewards do not necessarily have to be financial for them to be motivational. Different people respond in different ways to the various incentives that an organisation can offer.

- It is important to remember that what motivates you may very well be different from that which motivates your workforce. You need to be able to walk in other people's shoes.

- The key to successful team-building exercises is to ensure they are designed in such a way as to recognise the individual strengths and weaknesses of all the delegates.

- Motivational posters may be a corporate cliché – but, whilst they might sometimes seem a little silly, they do in fact work and so you should seriously consider using them.

10
Networking and socialising

So what exactly is this mysterious business of 'networking'?

It's a term that most people will be familiar with but it's often not clear what it really means. Many people think it sounds like the sort of activity that only the top brass and the sales team are likely to need to get up to over extravagant business lunches in expensive restaurants. Not true. Everyone needs to network. If you prefer, just think of it as socialising – but in a business sense. Everyone knows they need to socialise! And everyone should know they need to network.

As you meet new people – and make an effort to meet new people and to develop professional relationships with them – you will develop your network, a linked structure of individuals and a very valuable resource to you in numerous different ways.

In the previous chapters, I have talked about the people you work with on a daily basis. It is also important to build relationships beyond these people – and that's where networking comes in.

Getting ready to network

Networking requires a diverse range of skills and abilities. There's nothing inherently difficult about networking but I'd suggest you take the time to read through the first few sections of Chapter 13, Communication, in particular my comments about body language. Elements of Chapter 4, D-Day – your first day, are also relevant, for example how to make a powerful first impression, how to handle nerves and anxiety – and also how not to put your foot in it!

Creating and building rapport with people are essential – and one of the keys to this is empathy. Your success in networking will be determined by your degree of emotional intelligence – but fortunately that's something we can all work on and develop!

- Be genuine with other people; gain their trust and respect. Demonstrate sensitivity.

- Ask open-ended questions. You'll extract a lot more useful information.

- Listen to their answers, reading their body language and emotional cues.

Networking in person

We'll be talking about meetings later in this book – and meetings are, funnily enough, an excellent opportunity to meet new people and further develop your relationships with those you've already met, ie they're an excellent networking opportunity – and one of the commonest opportunities available to most people.

However, in the 'offline' world (we'll come to online networking in just a second), conferences, trade fairs and shows, exhibitions and other such events are undoubtedly the very best networking opportunities. The single most important reason that people are there is, quite simply, to network. You might encounter some resistance trying to network at a meeting but, when it comes to conferences and trade shows, it's precisely what other attendees will be expecting you to do.

You might not attend many such events but do be prepared to make the very most of them. Aim to meet as many people as possible; this is all about making an initial approach and then, subsequently, building on that relationship. Collect business cards as if your life depended on it! Taking a large folder (or briefcase) with you is also advisable, to help you cope physically with the quantity of corporate literature that will inevitably be thrust your way.

In the space of a few hours you could have the opportunity to talk face to face with dozens of different people. If you have business cards, make sure you take a plentiful supply with you. And, if you don't have any business cards, then ask your employer whether they can supply some. Reports of the death of the business card are greatly exaggerated; it is and will remain for some time to come an essential tool for the effective networker.

Another excellent opportunity for developing your network is provided through any off-the-job training you undertake – courses, workshops and seminars. You should always be on the lookout to identify opportunities to further expand and develop your network. They're everywhere. For example, my marketing director is a dab hand at making friends with people she's sitting next to on trains and planes when travelling on business. She'll even select her seat on a train according to the look of the person she'll be seated next to!

Networking takes many different forms and, for some people, it's almost an art form!

Networking online

You will most likely be familiar with Facebook. Facebook is simply a social networking tool – generally limited to social and not professional relationships. The king of business networking online is LinkedIn and your first step in networking online should therefore be to create your LinkedIn profile. A LinkedIn profile is very different from a CV but it's becoming equally important. LinkedIn is growing at a phenomenal rate and becoming an essential part of everyone's networking strategy.

Never seen LinkedIn?! Have a look at my LinkedIn profile and you'll see what I mean: **www.linkedin.com/in/jamesinnes**.

It's important to get a good balance when writing your LinkedIn profile – to get the right 'angle'. You need to be professional and yet still reveal a bit of personality. You also need to be careful to use the right keywords so that your profile succeeds in the search results.

Ten top tips to better networking

Before embarking on a networking campaign, take the time to read through, absorb and inwardly digest the following top 10 tips:

1   Prepare an 'elevator pitch' (60 seconds or so) which sums up coherently, concisely – and impressively – who you are and what you do.

2   Be positive and enthusiastic. Make a powerful first impression on everyone you meet. You want them to remember you – and for the right reasons, not the wrong ones!

3   Remember that a good networker has two ears but only one mouth – and uses them proportionately.

4   Don't spend an excessive amount of time networking with people you already know well; there's always greater value in making new contacts and building your network.

5 Keep careful records of the people you meet, who they are, what they do, what else you know about them – and how to contact them.

6 Connect online via LinkedIn with new contacts you meet offline. LinkedIn will do a lot of your record keeping for you.

7 Maintain contact with people you've met, whether you've met them physically or online. Nurture new relationships and further develop existing ones.

8 Be very careful not to harass people unnecessarily. You don't want to get a reputation for being overly pushy. It'll just turn people off. Strike a careful balance.

9 Bear in mind that it's not just people within your own network that you're interested in; it's also the individual networks of the people within your network.

10 Don't just take from your network. Make sure you give back as well. Become an important and useful resource for people in your network. What goes around comes around.

Using your network

Once you've developed your network you will find that you can put it to use in many different ways. Your network will be there as a resource for advice and guidance in numerous different respects, from identifying training opportunities through to coping with problems you're facing, for example when you're dealing with organisational change. It will help you to recognise and create opportunities, both directly related to your current role and also in a broader sense. Ultimately, it'll also be very useful in your search for your next job. Networking is – and always has been – a valuable job-hunting technique; I hired someone just yesterday as a result of their applying through a mutual contact. Networking works!

Summary

- There's nothing mysterious about networking; just think of it as socialising – but in a business sense.

- Make an effort to meet new people and to develop professional relationships with them so as to develop your network.

- Creating and building rapport with people is essential – and one of the keys to this is empathy.

- Your success in networking will be determined by your degree of emotional intelligence – but fortunately that's something we can all work on and develop!

- Be positive and enthusiastic. Make a powerful first impression on everyone you meet. You want them to remember you – and for the right reasons, not the wrong ones!

- In the offline world, conferences, trade fairs and shows, exhibitions and other such events are undoubtedly the very best networking opportunities.

- The single most important reason that people are there is, quite simply, to network.

- Another excellent opportunity for developing your network is provided through any off-the-job training you undertake – courses, workshops and seminars.

- You should always be on the lookout to identify opportunities to further expand and develop your network. They're everywhere.

- The king of business networking online is LinkedIn and your first step in networking online should therefore be to create your LinkedIn profile.

- Connect online via LinkedIn with new contacts you meet offline. LinkedIn will do a lot of your record keeping for you.

- Maintain contact with people you've met, whether you've met them physically or online. Nurture new relationships and further develop existing ones.

- Your network will be a resource for advice and guidance. It will help you to recognise and create opportunities and, ultimately, it'll also be very useful in your search for your next job.

PART FOUR
THE LEARNING CURVE

11

Planning and organisation

Before you can set about planning and organising your new workload, you need to be clear about what it is that you are planning and organising. Your first step is therefore to establish precisely what your various goals in your new job are – and what their respective priorities are.

'To Do' lists

For many people, the single most important tool in planning and organisation is a comprehensive list and/or schedule of what work actually needs to be done, generally called a 'To Do' list.

You should always have a To Do list – and maybe even several. You could have a master list accompanied by several sub-lists, each representing a different major task or project on your master list, broken up into smaller and more manageable chunks. You should also aim to have daily, weekly and/or monthly To Do lists setting out clearly what it is that you wish to – or need to – achieve on any one particular day or during the course of the week or month ahead.

Everyone is different but I personally find the best time to prepare the list for the day ahead is at the end of the previous day. Others may prefer to draw it up first thing in the morning before starting their day. It doesn't matter; whatever suits you best. The important thing is that it should enable you to see at a glance precisely what you need to achieve and, in this way, you should be better able to prioritise your workload and stay in control.

This is a technique that you should be employing immediately in your first few days on the job. Aim to start using To Do lists right from the start.

Priorities

Items on your To Do lists should preferably be listed in order of priority (certainly on your master list) so that you can clearly view tasks in order of importance. It is also a good idea to make sure that the list focuses on tasks which can only be carried out by yourself – or that you wish to carry out yourself – so that you are not wasting your time with work that could be delegated to others. (More on delegation in the next chapter…)

The list should also have scope for flexibility; it may expand (or contract!) and the priority of tasks may also change as the projects you are working on evolve. An up-to-date list will ensure that you can see at a glance what you need to do next and help ensure you tackle the most important tasks first, in turn enabling you to feel in control of your workload and helping to reduce the stress of starting your new job.

Some people also suggest preparing the To Do list in such a way as to put the more complicated (and therefore often more unpleasant!) tasks at the top of the list with the easier tasks towards the bottom. If you find you work best in the morning then this is a good strategy. If, like me, you're not a morning person then it's perhaps best to ease yourself into the day with some of the simpler tasks and then tackle the more significant ones in the afternoon once you're fully awake!

But don't be tempted to pick random tasks from the list, ie work through your list in order of preference. This will simply undermine the effective work structure which the list has helped you to create.

The difference between important and urgent

When setting your priorities in your new job it is important to be aware of the distinction between important and urgent. They're not necessarily the same thing.

All of your tasks will fall into one of two categories – those which are time dependent and those which aren't, ie those which have specific deadlines and those which don't.

You may have an important task ahead of you – but with no deadline. It is therefore not time dependent and cannot be urgent.

You may have a less important task ahead of you – but with a specific deadline for it to be actioned by. It is therefore time dependant and, depending on when that deadline is, it may or may not be urgent.

Which is the greater priority?

Generally, I would advise that you focus on tasks according to their level of importance. However, for the proportion of your workload which is time dependent, it is vital not to miss those deadlines. So concentrate on the important tasks but keep a careful eye on upcoming deadlines for time-dependent tasks, tackling them in time to ensure that those deadlines are not missed.

Any one task might of course 'migrate' from being not dependent on time to being time dependent (but rarely in the opposite direction). You may have no specific deadline for a particular task or project but, as time passes and you find you've been unable to complete it due to other conflicting priorities, it may become increasingly urgent, necessitating that you allocate a deadline to it. This highlights the need to regularly review your To Do lists, revising the priorities of particular items as necessary.

Maintaining your focus

Your To Do list should be seen as a tool for structuring and prioritising your workload, so try not to be demoralised if you do not complete every task on the list – the aim is to focus on high-priority work and to complete other tasks when time allows. These days, the modern workplace being what it is, it is generally a physical impossibility in many jobs to ever complete everything on your list – and I'd imagine this will most likely be the case in your new job. But don't let this get you down! The Pareto principle (better known as the 80–20 rule) means that the majority of items on your list will only account for a minority of your overall productivity – and many of them probably don't really matter at all. You will often find that tasks without specific deadlines which lurk around the bottom of a list will eventually cease to be necessary and can be removed.

But don't forget the satisfaction of being able to cross off the tasks that you have indeed successfully completed with a big, fat marker pen!

Get yourself straight

Successful planning and organisation in your new job start with the little things.

When you begin your new job, you must ensure you have everything you need at your desk – calculator, highlighters, etc – and, if you don't, then establish who it is you need to see to get such supplies.

Take time to have a look round your new computer. Get a new user ID and password if necessary; tidy up your desktop; file away (no, don't just throw away!) old files belonging to your predecessor; check out the software packages available to you and seek assistance if there's anything you're unfamiliar with.

You'll also need to make sure you're set up with an e-mail address if appropriate. Employers frequently overlook this when taking on a new recruit; don't hesitate to remind them.

Get comfortable in your new work environment. Is your chair, for example, correctly adjusted? Back and hand/wrist problems due to incorrect working postures account for a considerable amount of the time people take off sick. If you have any back problems then consider asking your new employer if they could supply (or if they'd mind if you supplied) a chair that would be better suited to your needs. Good employers take such matters seriously and should be only too happy to oblige. You may also wish to contemplate wrist support for your keyboard and an anti-glare filter for your monitor.

Achieving your goals

It's one thing to have planned and to be organised in your new job; it's another to make best use of your time to ensure your goals are met. That, to my mind, is by far the greater challenge. And it will be the subject of the next chapter.

Summary

- Before you can set about planning and organising your workload, you need to be clear about what it is that you are planning and organising.

- For many people, the single most important tool in planning and organisation is the To Do list.

- Items on your To Do lists should preferably be listed in order of priority (certainly on your master list) so that you can clearly view tasks in order of importance.

- The list should also have scope for flexibility; it may expand (or contract!) and the priority of tasks may also change as the projects you are working on evolve.

- Don't be tempted to pick random tasks from the list, ie work through your list in order of preference. This will simply undermine the effective work structure which the list has helped you to create.

- Concentrate on important tasks but keep a careful eye on upcoming deadlines for less important but time-dependent tasks.

- Regularly review your To Do lists, revising the priorities of particular items as necessary.

- Try not to be demoralised if you do not complete every task on the list – the aim is to focus on high-priority work and to complete other tasks when time allows.

- Don't forget the satisfaction of being able to cross off the tasks that you have indeed successfully completed with a big, fat marker pen!

- Ensure you have everything you need at your desk – calculator, highlighters, etc – and, if you don't, then establish who it is you need to see to get such supplies.

- Make sure you're set up with an e-mail address if appropriate. Employers frequently overlook this when taking on a new recruit; don't hesitate to remind them.

12
Time management

Arguably the most successful achievers across all industry sectors and professions are those who have learnt to manage their time effectively. If you can more effectively manage your daily workload, you will be able to increase your productivity whilst also ensuring you are able to maintain a healthy work–life balance. This is very important in your new job; get it right from the start.

Time management is not necessarily a fixed series of systems and procedures which apply to everyone – indeed, certain techniques that some people rely on simply do not suit other people. The key is to find a system that works for you at the outset of your new job – and to stick to it.

To achieve successful time management you will need to put into place certain procedures but, most importantly, effective time management is a frame of mind. Be conscious of your level of productivity and, if you see time being lost or wasted, then take steps to correct that. You should soon find that you are much more productive than before and that you waste far less time on trivial, unimportant and unnecessary tasks.

Procrastination

It was the English poet, Edward Young, who first put pen to paper to say, 'Procrastination is the thief of time'. And he was absolutely right. If you put off making critical decisions or completing complex tasks you can end up wasting a very significant amount of your valuable time. Many people delay certain tasks because they do not feel in the right frame of mind to tackle them or because they are waiting for a more suitable time. However, this can mean that these particular tasks are never completed – the 'right time' or 'right' frame of mind invariably never coming around.

Your To Do list is a key method of avoiding procrastination, as long as you have prioritised your list correctly. Another effective way of dealing with procrastination is to take some action regarding the task as soon as you think about it – at the very least entering it in its correct position of priority on your To Do list. It can also help to put the work in front of you so that you then have to make a conscious decision as to whether to put it back into the in-tray for another time or actually deal with it then and there.

If you've had problems with procrastination in the past then knock this issue on the head when starting your new job. Procrastination is one of the worst enemies of effective time management.

Just say no!

It is tempting to feel that you should always be prepared to accept every single task that is handed to you by your manager or created for you to deal with by your junior colleagues, particularly when you're starting a new job and you're keen as Tabasco sauce to impress – but this need not be the case. It is, of course, important to remain flexible so that you continue to perform well and give a good impression to your seniors, as well as providing support to your junior staff. But it is also, once again, a case of prioritising the additional tasks you are asked to fulfil, and knowing when one of them can wait until another time.

So how exactly do you turn down extra work without upsetting or offending anyone or making yourself look bad and giving a poor first impression to your new colleagues? Don't just say, 'No, I'm too busy!' That's not going to create a good impression, nor is it likely to have the desired effect. Your manager will probably still try to pressurise you into taking it on. You should instead explain and justify why you 'have' to say no. Don't be apologetic about it. Don't make it sound like you're making excuses. You're simply stating a fact.

Ascertain the nature of what you have been asked to complete, assess its level of urgency and maybe even suggest someone else who may be more suited to the task.

Here are a few examples to help get you thinking:

- 'Realistically, it's just not going to be possible for me to take this on, given the deadlines I'm up against on other fronts.'

- 'Because of my other commitments, I think I'm probably not the best person for this particular task right now. I'd suggest…'

- 'I'm afraid this would inevitably have to wait quite a while due to other more pressing priorities.'

- 'Whilst I'd love to help you out, I have to complete what I'm working on here by tomorrow.'

- 'Unfortunately, accepting this would mean that the project I'm currently working on becomes delayed.'

- 'Yes, but it'd have to be next month now. I'm booked solid for this month.'

That last example is a sneaky way of saying no by saying yes! But, generally, you will find that the more you continue to say yes when other people try to allocate their work to you, the more they will do this in the future, so it's important not to set such precedents when starting your new job. Just say no!

Delegation

An excellent way of subtly saying no is delegation. If you have people to whom you can reliably delegate a task – and within whose job function it is to carry out such a task – then delegate it! So much time is lost by handling tasks which would be best delegated to someone else.

The perfectionists amongst us often have considerable difficulty with delegation. Perfectionists tend to fear that a task, once delegated, simply won't be carried out to an appropriately high standard. This may be true – but does it actually matter? Whilst perfection is always highly desirable, it's often not very practical. Does the task have to be carried out perfectly? (And who defines perfection, anyway?) Or does it just have to be carried out sufficiently well that it doesn't lead to any problems? When juggling a heavy workload – as you most likely will be when starting your new job – you have to know when to say no to perfection and accept a compromise. There just aren't enough hours in the day – or days in the week!

Other fears associated with delegation include having difficulty in passing on responsibility to someone else (but isn't that the very definition of 'management'?) and worrying that someone else will receive the credit for the work – and yet everyone knows that managers generally receive full credit for the success of their subordinates. It's a manager's job to delegate and to supervise that delegation; it's not possible – or desirable – to do everything yourself single-handedly.

There is also the fear that if you delegate in order to save time, you may spend more time explaining how to carry out the task than it would have taken you to complete it yourself. That's a judgement issue. You have to weigh up how long it will take to explain to someone else to undertake the task compared with how long it would take to just do it yourself. Small one-off tasks are typically best done yourself but lengthier tasks – or tasks which are likely to need to be repeated in the future – are often best delegated. Set up an effective delegation strategy when starting your new job and you'll save yourself countless hours in the long run.

You should also bear in mind that the person to whom you are delegating may well appreciate the trust you are showing in them and, with appropriate supervision, they may well be able to undertake the task to the same high standards you have set for yourself. People can only really learn by doing something new.

It's important to note that you won't always delegate to someone who is your junior. Delegation to your peers – or even to your boss – can be necessary, depending on the circumstances. How you handle delegation to someone who is not your subordinate may require a slightly different approach – but the basic principles remain the same. Don't let your nervousness in your new job hold you back from delegation to either your peers or your boss; if it's the right call then make it!

Dealing with the unexpected

Possibly some of the most disruptive influences to your daily work schedule are those unexpected telephone calls, e-mails or visitors which no To Do list can fend off. This is why it is important to make sure that you do set aside a certain amount of time in the day for these sorts of interruptions. Although they are unavoidable, there are ways of decreasing their impact on your day.

If you receive telephone calls which you do not have time to deal with right away, explain you are very busy at present but would like to discuss the matter in hand and arrange a more suitable time to speak to the caller. In this way they will not feel you are cold-shouldering them, simply that you would like to speak to them when you can give them your full attention and are fully armed with any facts you may need to make full use of the discussion. If you are particularly busy, you could even ask your PA, secretary or receptionist to hold all calls and take detailed messages so that you can then allocate a block of time to returning calls, again fully prepared with all the facts you need.

And if someone comes to your office at an inconvenient time, a useful trick is to stand up immediately and stay standing – this tends to put people off from sitting down and generally makes the visit reach a conclusion much sooner. Try it and see! Make arrangements for another meeting with them at a time and location that suit you better.

Don't let unexpected interruptions have a negative impact on your ability to succeed in your new role.

Multi-tasking

Many busy people will claim to 'multi-task' to help them get done all that needs to be done. However, I must caution that research has shown that people just appear to be handling more than one task at the same time – and that multi-tasking is largely counterproductive, the lack of attention given to any one particular task resulting in (a) that task taking longer than it would otherwise have done and (b) that task being more prone to errors, errors which then consume more time (albeit perhaps later on) to be corrected. Greater efficiency is actually achieved by being able to concentrate fully on one task at a time.

Of course, there are times when we have no choice but to multi-task. You're busy writing up a report when an important and urgent e-mail pops up on your computer and, simultaneously, a colleague steps up to your desk to have a 'quick word' about something. But don't delude yourself into thinking that being able to multi-task all the time is in any way desirable as a form of time management. In the above scenario, you may be able to cope with the three different tasks demanding your attention but (a) you'll inevitably lose your train of thought to a degree for the report you're writing, (b) you'll most likely find yourself reading the e-mail more than once because your brain failed to take it in fully the first time and (c) your colleague will only get a cursory acknowledgement of what they're saying to you because half your brain is still writing your report and the other half is trying to respond to an e-mail! (Actually, that's not strictly accurate; experiments show that your brain acts as a whole and can only handle one task at a time…)

The above applies to men, just as much as it does to women. There is, as yet, no formal scientific evidence that women are any more capable of multi-tasking than men are. Only multi-core computers (which are essentially computers with more than one 'brain') are truly capable of multi-tasking!

Activity logs

We've covered the importance of the To Do list in the previous chapter. Another very useful document that you can prepare for yourself is an 'activity log'. This differs from a To Do list in that it details what you have actually achieved during the day, rather than what you set out to achieve. It is almost like keeping a diary of everything you do, and when you do it. It can be very useful in enabling you to see when you are at your most productive. It can also highlight times in the day when you are just wasting time. Your activity log can even be used in conjunction with your To Do list so that the more urgent tasks are completed at the times of the day when you perform better.

Using an activity log can also be a useful motivational technique. At the end of each day, write down your greatest achievement of the day. It's all so easy for us to focus on what we haven't done rather than what we have done – when we've normally done far more than we think. As you flick back through your activity logs for your first few weeks in your new job and read through your daily achievements, you'll realise just how much you've actually already accomplished – and it'll help you to get a clearer idea of what really matters in your work compared to what is just trivial and incidental.

Clear out the clutter

Laurence J Peter said, 'If a cluttered desk is the sign of a cluttered mind, what is the significance of a clean desk?' I'll let you think about that one…

Whilst some people seem to thrive when surrounded by clutter, most people perform best when they're not surrounded by clutter – and yet most people are indeed surrounded by clutter! Whilst not exactly a time management technique as such, aim to keep your desk as clear (and clean!) as possible. Throw out the rubbish. Chuck away unwanted paperwork. Bin the executive desk toy. It is very hard to be a successful time manager if you are constantly sifting through mounds of clutter on your desk.

The same applies equally – if not more so – to your computer desktop and to your e-mail inbox. Keep them as uncluttered as possible. File away all those random files you've got stored on your desktop – and delete all the temporary ones you no longer need! As for your e-mail, set up a sub-folder system into which you can categorise incoming e-mail as, for example, 'High priority', 'Low priority' and 'Very low priority', leaving just items which need to be actioned immediately in your main inbox. ('Very low priority', by the way, is just code for 'Bin' and is where you should store all the fascinating newsletters, etc that you really think you should be reading through from A to Z but just don't seem to be able to find the time to do so…)

Relax; take it easy

It should be noted that managing your time effectively doesn't necessarily mean working every single minute of it. Quite the contrary. It is vital to allow time for relaxation, even if it is only a few minutes of quiet time with the telephone off the hook and the door to your office closed. Most people respond better to a heavy workload if they have had some time to themselves. Everybody has different levels of ability as to how long they can concentrate for without taking a break – and without losing their focus. But everyone has a limit. Know what your limits are and schedule in appropriate breaks, even if it's just to step outside the building for a few minutes and get some fresh air. You will impress people in your new job by the results you achieve, not by being chained to your desk 24 hours a day!

Summary

- If you can more effectively manage your daily workload, you will be able to increase your productivity whilst also ensuring you are able to maintain a healthy work–life balance.

- Procrastination is the thief of time. If you put off making critical decisions or completing complex tasks you can end up wasting a very significant amount of your valuable time.

- If you have people to whom you can reliably delegate a task – and within whose job function it is to carry out such a task – then delegate it!

- It's a manager's job to delegate and to supervise that delegation; it's not possible – or desirable – to do everything yourself single-handedly.

- Small one-off tasks are typically best done yourself but lengthier tasks – or tasks which are likely to need to be repeated in the future – are often best delegated.

- Delegation to your peers – or even to your boss – can be necessary, depending on the circumstances.

- Research has shown that multi-tasking is largely counterproductive. Greater efficiency is actually achieved by being able to concentrate fully on one task at a time.

- At the end of each day, write down your greatest achievement of the day. It's a very useful motivational technique.

- Aim to keep your desk as clear (and clean!) as possible. Throw out the rubbish. Chuck away unwanted paperwork. Bin the executive desk toy.

- Set up a sub-folder system into which you can categorise incoming e-mail as, for example, 'High priority', 'Low priority' and 'Very low priority'.

- It is vital to allow time for relaxation, even if it is only a few minutes of quiet time with the telephone off the hook and the door to your office closed.

13
Communication

Establishing and maintaining effective channels of communication with your boss, with your colleagues and with anyone else you may work with – customers, suppliers, etc – are imperative in your new job.

Successful communication is all about building relationships, avoiding misunderstandings and enhancing productivity through the clear exchange of ideas. It clarifies thoughts, promotes understanding and leads to action. And it is worth noting that communication involves both speaking and listening so that mutual understanding is achieved.

Body language

Many experts agree that much of what we communicate when we communicate verbally isn't actually verbal; it's physical. Only a small minority of what we communicate is communicated by the actual words we say. Much more is communicated by the volume, pitch and rhythm of our voice and even more via our body language, in particular our facial expressions.

STATISTIC

Research suggests that no more than 30 per cent and maybe as little as 7 per cent of what we communicate is communicated via our words themselves.

Everyone is inherently sensitive to certain nuances of body language. It's instinctive and its importance should not be underestimated. The human ability to communicate via language may only have evolved as little as 50,000 years ago and yet we were clearly able to communicate with each other prior to that. Body language predates verbal language by a very long time and, whilst we might not be consciously aware of it, it remains our most significant form of communication.

Negative body language

There are, of course, certain elements of body language you should avoid. Some are obvious: You shouldn't pick your nails, pick your nose – or pick any other bodily part for that matter!

And some are less obvious...

Here are some examples of negative traits and how your body language can give them away:

- defensiveness: crossing your arms;

- boredom: feet tapping, playing with your pen, looking down, slouching;

- nervousness: fidgeting, thumb-twiddling, playing with your hair;

- arrogance/overconfidence: hands clasped behind head;

- aggression: postures such as hands on hips and pointing or wagging your index finger;

- doubt: rubbing eyes or nose.

I once had a manager (who shall remain unnamed) who seemed incapable of talking to anyone without his hands either clasped behind his head or on his hips. He was ostensibly communicating confidence but it was easy to see through him and to realise what he was actually communicating was a lack of confidence.

Reading others' body language

Others' body language can give you some insight into what they think of what you are saying – for example if they're getting bored! You can then react to that, for example by changing the subject fast!

TOP TIP

An 'insider' trick is to copy certain aspects of someone's body language. Imitating someone else's body language can have a positive subconscious effect on their impression of you. The theory is that they will feel you are on the same wavelength as them and automatically become better disposed towards you. You should try to be subtle about it, of course – and avoid copying any negative behaviour!

Tone of voice

In verbal communication, your tone of voice is very important. Nerves, stress and pressure will all reflect in the way you speak – so will confidence, enthusiasm and energy. Nerves, stress and pressure will have a negative impact, whilst confidence, enthusiasm and energy will come across positively.

Take some time to work on your tone of voice. You might feel a little mad talking aloud to the mirror but it's an exercise that's well worth trying!

Eye contact

Eye contact is critical to effective communication. Make and maintain eye contact – without actually staring! Eye contact is essential when trying to convey trust and confidence but should not be overdone as it can come across as aggressive. But, once you've established eye contact, people are a lot more likely to listen to what you have to say.

The telephone

Communicating by telephone is not really that different from communicating face to face. The main difference is that you won't, of course, have any visual cues – and neither will the other person. Issues such as body language are immediately irrelevant but other factors, such as tone of voice, become more important to compensate.

In particular, you need to concentrate on articulating clearly and getting your tone of voice right. The other person might not be able to see you smiling but they'll be able to hear it in your voice – and they'll also be able to hear a frown!

Do be careful of background noises and try to conduct your telephone conversations somewhere calm and quiet, rather than on a busy street corner! You should especially avoid eating, drinking, smoking or chewing gum during a telephone conversation – as all of these will be distinctly audible. The only exception to this would be for you to take an occasional sip of water to stop your mouth drying up.

> When I was very much younger than I am today I allowed myself to be interviewed by telephone with my rather rude African Grey parrot within earshot! And one indignant interviewer reported to a survey that he once had a candidate flush the lavatory on him during a telephone interview!

Videoconferencing and webcams

More and more organisations are looking to harness tools such as videoconferencing and the Internet to facilitate communications.

If meeting in person is impractical (or, for whatever reason, undesirable) then you might find yourself expected to handle this form of communication – and it might not have been an issue in your previous jobs.

First and foremost, you need to ensure you fully understand how to use the technology in question. It will not create a good impression if you struggle to deal with the technology.

Apart from this, there's very little difference from normal face-to-face communication. You will be in full view, so maintain a reasonable level of eye contact, smile, articulate clearly – and behave precisely as you would if you were meeting in person.

Because you will be responsible for controlling your own environment, make sure that nobody disturbs you. If somebody walks in on you then it is going to reflect very badly on you. This also means switching mobile phones to silent mode and taking other phones off the hook.

E-mail

You may still use the post – and fax is still used very occasionally – but the vast majority of written communication these days is by e-mail.

There are certain practicalities which you should take into account when sending an e-mail:

Subject line: Never leave it blank! It's extremely unprofessional to do so. But do keep it short and simple and easy to understand. And be careful in your choice of words; you certainly don't want to risk your e-mail being labelled as spam and discarded.

Form of address: Just because this is an e-mail is no reason to start with 'Hi', or suchlike. Start your e-mail just as you would start a proper, professional letter. This isn't an e-mail to a pal.

Signature: Many people have an automated e-mail 'signature' which goes out at the bottom of every e-mail they send. This is a very good idea; if you don't have one then consider implementing one.

Cc and Bcc: Think carefully before including contacts in the Cc or Bcc fields. Also, before hitting 'Reply all' on an e-mail, ask yourself whether it's really necessary – or desirable – for everyone who received the original e-mail to receive your reply.

Attachments: There are two points to note here: (a) if you say you're including an attachment then don't forget to attach it and (b) make sure you attach the correct file! It sounds obvious but these are both incredibly common mistakes – and they don't make a good impression on the reader.

Forwarding: Think carefully before forwarding someone's e-mail on to someone else. How would they react if they knew? Is there any earlier correspondence further down the e-mail 'thread' that the new recipient should perhaps not be seeing?!

Content: E-mail is so easy to send. Never send an e-mail when you're angry. And never send an e-mail which includes anything you wouldn't want your boss or the media to see.

Accuracy: Because it's so immediate, people are often less careful about spelling and grammar when writing an e-mail. People are also very reliant on automatic spell checkers to pick up any mistakes for them. Make sure your e-mails are of the highest quality by carefully reading through them before you send them so you can correct any spelling or grammatical errors.

English is, of course, the main international business language, yet, for the majority of people using it, it isn't their first language. In the next chapter I shall therefore be covering some key spelling and grammatical issues.

Summary

- Establishing and maintaining effective channels of communication with your boss, with your colleagues and with anyone else you may work with – customers, suppliers, etc – are imperative.

- Successful communication is all about building relationships, avoiding misunderstandings and enhancing productivity through the clear exchange of ideas.

- Communication involves both speaking and listening so that mutual understanding is achieved.

- Everyone is inherently sensitive to certain nuances of body language. It's instinctive and its importance should not be underestimated.

- Take some time to work on your tone of voice. You might feel a little mad talking aloud to the mirror but it's an exercise that's well worth trying!

- Eye contact is critical to effective communication. Make and maintain eye contact – without actually staring!

- An 'insider' trick is to copy certain aspects of someone's body language. Imitating someone else's body language can have a positive subconscious effect on their impression of you.

- Avoid eating, drinking, smoking or chewing gum during a telephone conversation – all of these will be distinctly audible.

- E-mail is so easy to send. Never send an e-mail when you're angry. And never send an e-mail which includes anything you wouldn't want your boss or the media to see.

14
Writing skills

The ability to write good English is a much sought-after skill in the workplace.

The vast majority of documents contain at least one linguistic error. However, whilst spelling and grammatical errors are clearly detrimental to your written correspondence – and irritating to the reader – they should be easily avoidable. The answer is to check, check and check again – and then, depending on the nature of the document, have someone else check for good measure!

Reading through the document yourself is clearly essential, but having a friend or colleague read it through can be an even better idea – because it's so easy to miss mistakes in your own work when you've been staring at it for hours. (This even applies to professional writers!)

English is the international language of business. However, by definition, for most of the people who need to write in English, it won't be their first language. In this chapter, I'll cover some key spelling and grammatical issues which should be of interest to anyone starting out in a new job using the English language. Even native speakers make plenty of mistakes.

Commonly misspelled words

Avoiding spelling errors is fundamental.

In one unfortunate case, the individual in question got very confused about the difference between 'role' and 'roll'. He kept referring throughout his report to the various 'rolls' in question, eg 'an important roll in the finance department', 'sharing a roll with a colleague', etc.

Any word can be misspelled, even 'misspelled' itself! However, some words are very frequently misspelled in business writing and these are the ones you should keep a particularly careful eye out for:

- separate – often seen spelled as 'seperate';

- necessary – neccesary, necessery, nesessary;

- liaising – most commonly misspelled as 'liasing';

- liaison – likewise misspelled as 'liason';

- personnel – personnell, personell, personel.

Easily confused words

There are also various 'pairs' of words which I commonly see used incorrectly that I'd like to draw to your attention. It can be a little complicated so, if you get at all confused, I suggest you get out the dictionary!

principle/principal
'The principal problem you might face with a new project is that you don't agree, in principle, with the approach the management wants you to take.'
'Principle' is a noun, commonly referring to a personal belief or conviction, eg 'It's against my principles.' Alternatively it can refer to how something works, eg 'The principle of a hot-air balloon is very simple.'
'Principal', however, can be both an adjective and a noun. As an adjective, it normally means first, main or chief, eg 'My principal objection is the cost.'
As a noun, however, it has a whole host of different meanings.

stationery/stationary
'You might be responsible for ordering stationery supplies from the stationer. However, if you're stuck in your car at the traffic lights then you're stationary!'
'Stationery' is a noun for writing materials – paper, pens, etc. 'Stationary' is an adjective which means not moving or standing still.

complement/compliment
'If you and a colleague successfully complete a project together then you might compliment each other on a job well done. Alternatively, if he possesses certain skills that you don't – and vice versa – then you might say that you complement each other.'
The two words have very different meanings.

arise/arouse
'A rude and abusive call centre worker could easily cause customer complaints to arise – and that might arouse a rather angry response from the management.'
Again, two words with different meanings.

'We must swiftly and effectively resolve any customer complaints which arouse.'

effect/affect

'You can effect a change and, depending on the circumstances, you can also
affect a change. However, whilst a change will have an effect, it can't have an
affect. And, whilst you might be affected by a change, you certainly can't be
effected by it.'

This is a complicated one!

advice/advise

'You might advise your clients not to sue the local newspaper but they might
decide to totally ignore your advice.'

'Advice' is a noun and 'advise' is a verb. They're not only different words;
they're also pronounced differently.

practice/practise

'You can work in a doctor's practice and you can put your ideas into practice but
if you want to deliver an outstanding presentation to a potential client then you
had better practise!'

Whilst pronounced the same, 'practice' is a noun and 'practise' is a verb.
In American English, 'practise' doesn't actually exist at all. Americans use
'practice' both as a noun and as a verb and this is just one of many
differences between British English and American English.

Let's take a closer look at the vagaries of our American cousins.

Across the pond...

The differences between British English and American English are numerous and
often cause confusion.

The bottom line is that if you're looking for work in the UK, clearly you should be
using British English spelling. However, if you're looking for work abroad, American
English may more commonly be used.

We've covered *practice/practise*. Here's another problematic pair: *licence/license*.

'Licence' is a noun in British English and 'license' is a verb. A driving examiner can
license you to drive – but the plastic card you'll get is your licence. Americans, on the
other hand, don't use the word 'licence' at all. They use 'license' both as a noun and
as a verb.

A particular problem is that word processing software (for example, Microsoft Word) is often, by default, set to American spelling rather than British English (because the software creators are normally American). It will therefore highlight some words as incorrect even when they're not – they're just British English spellings and not American spellings. This can in fact often be resolved by ensuring that the document is set to UK spelling.

In Microsoft Word 2010:

- Click on the 'File' tab.

- Click 'Options'.

- Click 'Language'.

- In the 'Set the Office Language Preferences' dialogue box, under 'Choose Editing Languages', select and click on 'English (United Kingdom)'.

- Click 'Set as Default'.

- Close all your Office 2010 programs and then open them again for the change to take effect.

For other word processing packages you can consult the user guide or use the built-in 'Help' facility. Failing that, you can find the solution online.

Fully capitalised words

Fully capitalised words are also a problem – because spell checks commonly ignore these. However, this is in fact only the default setting and can be changed.

In Microsoft Word 2010:

- Click on the 'File' tab.

- Click 'Options'.

- Click 'Proofing'.

- Uncheck the box next to 'Ignore words in UPPERCASE'.

The procedure in Microsoft Word 2007 is very similar; you will need to go to 'Review', then 'Spelling & Grammar', then 'Options'. And in Microsoft Word 2000/2003 you will need to go to 'Tools', then 'Options', then 'Spelling & Grammar'.

You also need to be careful with acronyms, eg ITV, RSPCA, HMRC, HTML, etc.

Typos

'Typos', or typographical errors, can be even harder to pick up on than plain spelling errors. A spell check won't pick up on mistakes such as 'extremely busty'! You may be surprised, but this sort of error is not unusual. Take a look at where the letters 't' and 'y' sit on a keyboard – right next to each other.

As well as adding in an extra letter, another common typo is to completely miss out a letter: 'in the opinion of the finance manger'.

> I've certainly seen some interesting job titles in people's CVs... I had one client who was a *Metal Health Advisor* and another who was looking for work as a *Diary Farmer*!

Freudian slips

A final type of spelling/typing error I'd like to cover is where the writer, for whatever reason, simply picks the wrong word.

These can be of the banal sort where you type 'their' instead of 'there' or 'your' instead of 'you're'. You know which is correct but your brain somehow sends a different message to the keyboard.

Alternatively, typos can be rather more interesting... One which immediately springs to my mind is the hopeful jobseeker who stated they were 'a conscious employee.' You'd hope so, really...

> Probably one of the 'best' typos I've seen was someone explaining that they were 'financially incompetent'!

You probably think I'm making all of this up but, trust me, it wouldn't be in this book if I hadn't actually seen it!

A spell check won't detect these sorts of problem – but your reader very possibly will.

Again, careful proofreading is the answer.

Punctuation

Errors in punctuation are the most common grammatical errors and, amongst these, the apostrophe is definitely the most abused. For example:

Londons' No. 1 retailer of kitchen appliances

Or, possibly even worse:

Londons No. 1 retailer of kitchen appliances

The correct usage is of course:

London's No. 1 retailer of kitchen appliances

If you're not sure what the rules are then there are plenty of articles on the Internet which explain correct punctuation in detail.

It's and *its* are also frequently misused. And you sometimes even see *its'* – which doesn't exist at all!

Remember that *it's* is a contraction of *it is*, whereas *its* is a possessive pronoun, eg 'When it's necessary, the computer will automatically update its antivirus software.'

Poor old apostrophes – so frequently mistreated. But it's not always black and white, of course. Whilst it is grammatically correct to say 'four years' experience', many people believe it should be 'four year's experience', so you might think it is better for you to make a deliberate error. The choice is yours. This is the only time I would ever consider recommending anything less than grammatical perfection!

Can you spot any spelling, grammatical or typographical errors in this book? We hope not! But, if you do, then please visit **www.ineedacv.co.uk/oops** to let us know, so we can correct it for the next edition.

Summary

- The ability to write good English is a much sought-after skill in the workplace.

- Spelling and grammatical errors are clearly detrimental to your written correspondence but they should be easily avoidable.

- The answer is to check, check and check again – and then, depending on the nature of the document, have someone else check for good measure!

- Reading through a document yourself is clearly essential, but having a friend or colleague read it through can be an even better idea.

- Avoiding spelling errors is fundamental. Any word can be misspelled, even 'misspelled' itself!

- The differences between British English and American English are numerous and often cause confusion.

- A particular problem is that word processing software (for example, Microsoft Word) is often, by default, set to American spelling rather than British English.

- Fully capitalised words are also a problem – because spell checks commonly ignore these.

15
Presentations

In many lines of work, the ability to give powerful presentations is a key skill – and, if this is a requirement in your new job, then it's an excellent opportunity to demonstrate your ability to organise yourself, plan, prepare and communicate effectively.

Preparation

In most circumstances, an employer will be decent enough to warn you that they want you to give a presentation. This gives you plenty of time to carry out any necessary research, write, memorise and practise your presentation.

TOP TIP

Make sure your presentation follows a clear and logical structure, beginning with a suitable introduction and closing with an appropriate conclusion; it's always the beginning and the ending of a presentation which get the most attention.

Usually you will be given a specific topic for the presentation as well as a suggested length – and it is, of course, essential to adhere to any such guidelines.

Nerves

Nerves are probably the biggest enemy you face when delivering a presentation, especially if you're nervous enough about starting your new job anyway. You're up there at the front all alone with everyone staring at you! It's a natural instinct for you to feel threatened by this and for your body to be pumped full of adrenaline – and adrenaline isn't your best friend when you're trying to give a successful presentation! It might have been useful hundreds of thousands of years ago when you were cornered by a sabre-toothed tiger, but now it'll just cause you to panic even more!

Here are my top 10 key tips for calming those nerves:

1 Stop thinking about yourself. Focus your attention on your audience.

2 Bear in mind that the audience is on your side and that they are not your enemy.

3 Try to imagine you're talking to each person individually, not as a group.

4 Ask rhetorical questions to reinforce the illusion that it's a one-on-one conversation.

5 Have a glass of water to sip from just in case your mouth (or brain!) dries up.

6 Take slower, deeper breaths. It'll calm you down and help get more oxygen to your brain.

7 Smile; it's a natural relaxant. And it'll make a good impression on your audience too.

8 Limit your caffeine intake; you definitely don't want to appear manic…

9 Visualise the end of the presentation and the round of applause you could be getting.

10 Ask yourself what's the worst that could happen; after all, it's just a presentation!

And here's one last idea for you. There's a famous interview technique whereby, to make yourself feel better, you imagine your interviewer sitting there in their underwear. It actually does work – and works equally well when you're giving a presentation. Just imagine your audience are all sitting there in their underwear. (Don't tell anyone – but I do this when I give presentations!)

TOP TIP

Speak confidently – slightly slower, slightly louder and slightly more deeply than you would normally do – and articulate each syllable clearly. Slowing down is particularly important and will, in itself, help you to calm down. Don't let your nerves win the battle – because it'll reflect immediately in your tone of voice.

Cue cards

Many presenters, myself included, rely on cue cards to help them through their presentation.

Reading from a script is totally unacceptable and, whilst you should make an effort to memorise as much of your presentation as possible, memorising it verbatim is likely to result in a fairly stiff and stilted delivery.

By using cue cards you can identify the next point you wish to make with a quick downwards glance, helping you to spend most of your time maintaining eye contact with your audience.

Eye contact

If you've got an audience in front of you then don't focus too much on any one person – move your gaze randomly around the room and aim to make brief eye contact with everyone. You may even find that they nod their head in agreement!

Physical gestures

Whilst it's normally fine to walk up and down a little bit – and it'll help to expend some of your excess nervous energy – you should avoid pacing the floor excessively. Likewise, it's fine to gesture with your hands – but try to keep it within reasonable limits. You want to convey the impression of someone who is calm and in control – even if you do have a swarm of butterflies in your stomach!

Visual aids

You should be notified in advance whether or not you are expected to use any visual aids – for example a PowerPoint slideshow. If it's not specified then there's nothing to be lost in asking – a PowerPoint presentation is always more powerful than a straightforward verbal presentation. It also gives you an opportunity to demonstrate your proficiency with PowerPoint.

Practice makes perfect

The secret to a successful presentation is practice. Practise reciting your presentation by yourself; practise in front of the mirror; practise in front of a friend.

The more you practise your presentation, the more confident you will become.

Q&A

As you finish your presentation, it is, of course, expected that you will ask your audience whether they have any questions. You should endeavour to anticipate the sort of questions you are likely to be asked and have rough answers prepared in advance.

Finally, it's always a nice touch to thank your audience for listening.

Summary

- Make sure your presentation follows a clear and logical structure, beginning with a suitable introduction and closing with an appropriate conclusion.

- Usually you will be given a specific topic for the presentation as well as a suggested length – and it is, of course, essential to adhere to any such guidelines.

- Don't let your nerves get the better of you – because it'll reflect immediately in your tone of voice.

- Speak confidently – slightly slower, slightly louder and slightly more deeply than you would normally do – and articulate each syllable clearly.

- By using cue cards you can identify the next point you wish to make with a quick downwards glance.

- Eye contact is essential to effective communication. Move your gaze randomly around the room and aim to make brief eye contact with everyone.

- The secret to a successful presentation is practice. The more you practise your presentation, the more confident you will become.

- Endeavour to anticipate the sort of questions your audience is likely to ask – and have rough answers prepared in advance.

16
Meetings

Attending a meeting is reasonably straightforward; organising, chairing and managing a meeting are much less so. This chapter will therefore focus on the latter.

Meetings, besides being an excellent way for you to meet and get to know people in your new job, should be ideal opportunities for brainstorming new initiatives, improving communication, increasing morale and motivation, resolving conflicts and problems and enhancing team cohesion. However, the reality can be somewhat different. Meetings are not always popular activities for those expected to attend because they can seem a tedious and irrelevant waste of time, eating into time which could have been spent upon existing workloads.

This chapter will show you how to chair successful meetings which are productive for all involved.

Establishing the purpose

When you are organising a meeting, your first consideration should be to ascertain exactly why the meeting is necessary. Without a clear purpose, you may find delegates are unwilling to attend or bored and demotivated if they do make it to the meeting. Successful meetings are purposeful, well planned and organised and lead to positive action being taken as a result.

Selecting the date, time and venue

If you want to see good attendance levels at your meeting, you will need to ensure the date is suitable for the key delegates and that its location is easily accessible to all. If possible, liaise with the delegates well in advance of the proposed date to try to ensure maximum attendance. However, whilst the schedule of your delegates is important, it may also be necessary to reiterate the importance, relevance and degree of urgency of the proposed meeting, so that delegates can reschedule other less urgent commitments if required.

If the meeting is a brief, internal affair, the venue you select will probably be within your own building or at a location close by. Alternatively, some meetings may be better suited to an external venue such as a hotel with conference facilities. If this is the case, the time you choose for the meeting will be dictated to some extent by the time it will take for the delegates to reach the venue. Additionally, the time you set for the conclusion of the meeting should allow for people to be able to get home at a reasonable hour. If many of the delegates have to travel some distance to reach the meeting, you may want to consider providing overnight accommodation on the eve of the meeting. This can help to build a rapport between the delegates whilst also allowing for an early start and, hopefully, a reasonable finishing time.

Set the agenda

To ensure the success of a meeting, it is important that there are a clear purpose and agenda. A list of exactly which objectives the meeting is intended to achieve should be prepared in advance and distributed to all delegates – along with details of when and where the meeting will take place and who else will be in attendance. This enables those attending to make any necessary preparations and to make notes of anything they wish to discuss in relation to the items on the agenda. It can be useful to provide estimates of timescales for each item on the agenda, so that delegates are aware of how much they can realistically contribute to the debate. Ideally, the most urgent items should be placed at the top of the agenda so as to ensure they are covered adequately before time runs out.

The proposed agenda should also invite delegates to submit any other topics they would like to discuss. In this way, new items from delegates can be included in the final agenda, whilst simultaneously eliminating the need to 'throw open' the meeting for other issues – something which can play havoc with even the best-planned agenda.

Prepare the venue

You should aim to arrive at the venue well in advance of the other delegates. This will enable you to ensure the layout is appropriate and that all necessary equipment and materials are in place. Generally, the number of people attending the meeting will dictate the seating arrangement. You can opt for rows of seats, a horseshoe layout or simply one long table in the centre of the room. Whichever format you choose, the position of the chairperson is imperative. Everybody in the audience needs to be able to clearly see the chairperson and any visual aids being used. All lighting and electrical equipment needs to be checked to ensure they are in full working order and projectors or flip charts need to be positioned appropriately.

If the meeting is being held at an external venue, you should make sure you have introduced yourself to the staff and confirmed that refreshments have been organised, if appropriate. It is also important to familiarise yourself with the locations of the toilets and emergency exits.

Once you are satisfied the venue has been set up correctly, you are then able to begin to create a productive working atmosphere by meeting and greeting the delegates and putting them at their ease as they arrive.

Opening the meeting

Ideally, the meeting should always start on time to ensure you have control of proceedings from the outset. It is, however, acceptable to put back the start of the meeting a little in the event of a key delegate being unavoidably delayed.

You should open the meeting by introducing yourself as the chair and by introducing the other delegates in attendance. Apologies should also be made for those who have been unable to attend. The purpose of the meeting should be reiterated, to ensure that everyone is focused on what you hope to achieve. Briefly run through the agenda, explain when breaks and any refreshments will be served and announce when you hope to have concluded the meeting by.

Controlling the meeting

The role of the chair is not only to ensure the meeting runs to schedule, but also to encourage all delegates to make a valuable contribution. Some people may feel uncomfortable voicing their opinions in front of a group and so it is the responsibility of the chair to spot body language which indicates a delegate has something they wish to add to the debate, but are reluctant to do so. The chair should also stimulate healthy debate on each item on the agenda, so that diverse ranges of opinions are heard before an item is concluded. It can also be useful to invite questions from delegates to make sure that everybody fully understands what has been discussed before moving on to the next item on the agenda.

It is of course possible that confrontations will take place in meetings and it also falls under the chair's remit to ensure that these are handled effectively and are not allowed to have too great an impact on the agenda. If necessary, try to move on to the next item on the agenda and, if appropriate, agree that a more detailed investigation can be carried out into the contentious issues after the meeting has been concluded.

Once each item on the agenda has been discussed, the whole meeting should be summarised and points that need to be followed up should be clarified. The chair is responsible for ensuring notes are taken throughout the meeting and that follow-up tasks are allocated appropriately. If necessary, a further meeting should be arranged before the meeting is brought to a close.

Follow up

The notes taken by the chair (or the chair's assistant) throughout the course of the meeting should be transcribed into clear and concise minutes for distribution to all those who attended, those who were not able to make it to the meeting, and all other relevant parties. All actions that were agreed upon should be emphasised with the person responsible for dealing with each one clearly named on the minutes. The chair should then ensure that all of these actions are completed in accordance with the deadlines that were agreed.

The success of subsequent meetings is likely to be dictated by the level of activity that followed the initial meeting. If action proposed in the meeting is rigorously followed up and positive action taken as a result of the meeting, delegates are likely to perceive future meetings as useful, meaningful events which aid their working life and productivity, rather than merely as an additional burden to their workload.

Summary

- Meetings should be ideal opportunities for brainstorming new initiatives, improving communication, resolving conflicts and problems and enhancing team cohesion.

- Meetings are not always popular activities for those expected to attend because they can seem a tedious and irrelevant waste of time.

- When you are organising a meeting, your first consideration should be to ascertain exactly why the meeting is necessary – to establish a clear purpose.

- Successful meetings are purposeful, well planned and organised and lead to positive action being taken as a result.

- If you want to see good attendance levels at your meeting, you will need to ensure the date is suitable for the key delegates and that the meeting's location is easily accessible to all.

- To ensure the success of a meeting, it is important that there are a clear purpose and agenda.

- You should aim to arrive at the venue well in advance of the other delegates to ensure the layout is appropriate and that all necessary equipment and materials are in place.

- The role of the chair is not only to ensure the meeting runs to schedule, but also to encourage all delegates to make a valuable contribution.

- The chair should also stimulate healthy debate on each item on the agenda, so that diverse ranges of opinions are heard before an item is concluded.

- Once each item on the agenda has been discussed, the whole meeting should be summarised and points that need to be followed up should be clarified.

- The chair is responsible for ensuring notes are taken throughout the meeting and that follow-up tasks are allocated appropriately.

- The chair should then ensure that all of these actions are completed in accordance with the deadlines that were agreed.

17
Remote working

Compelling workers to work from their employer's premises is now a much less prevalent employer philosophy and, in your new job, you may find yourself faced, possibly for the very first time, by the prospect of remote working.

In 2002, the UK government passed the Employment Act, stating that any employee with children under the age of six should have the right to request flexible working hours and that all employers should be obliged to give such requests serious consideration. (And many other countries have implemented similar legislation.) Since the introduction of this legislation, many more people have chosen to work from home with the aim of achieving the optimum work–life balance. Depending on your circumstances, even if your employer doesn't propose the possibility of remote working in your new job, you may wish to discuss the idea with them.

STATISTIC

Well over a million people in the UK work purely from home and nearly four million work largely from home.

Remote working doesn't suit all lines of work. It is clearly impossible for manufacturers and retailers. It is typically in the various 'service' sectors that remote working is most popular.

The advantages of working from home

There are a number of benefits of remote working, one of which is being able to minimise the time spent commuting and the expenses incurred as a result. This in turn can make the working day shorter, thus allowing people to have more free time to spend with their families. Also, working from home does allow greater flexibility to deal with any unexpected incidents that may occur throughout the day. This can lead to a generally happier employee, which in turn can often lead to increased productivity.

Employers offering flexible working practices are seen as particularly desirable by prospective employees and they can also enjoy increased staff retention and loyalty as a result. Increased levels of staff retention result in reduced costs in terms of recruitment and training of new staff members but there are also other significant cost benefits to remote working. For example, office space can be reduced, which will then have a positive impact on the organisation's overheads. Some employers operate a desk-share system whereby staff who regularly work at home do not have their own desk in the office but are allocated desk space as and when required.

There is also an environmental advantage to remote working in that the reduction in commuting will have a significant effect on carbon dioxide and nitrogen oxide emissions.

Sounds very much like a win–win situation, doesn't it?

How to make remote working a success

In order to make working from home possible, there are some important considerations for both you and your employer. The first of these is to ensure that the necessary technology is in place to enable effective remote working. Broadband technology and Virtual Private Networks (VPN) mean that employees can now have access to office systems from their home computers, whilst also offering employers the reassurance that their data remains secure. Voice over Internet Protocol (VoIP) means that employees can make business calls from their home telephones, which are charged to the organisation rather than to their own telephone bill.

Videoconferencing enables people in remote locations to communicate directly with each other, so even meetings with clients or colleagues can be conducted in the comfort of your own home without the need to travel.

Instant Messaging allows people working from home to keep in regular contact with their colleagues in the office so that they can seek support and assistance when required and can be kept updated with any important information. It also helps to fill in for that important social aspect.

Ten top tips for working from home

I personally spend a considerable amount of time working from home. I find I'm much more productive than in an office when it seems like every minute of every day somebody wants to interrupt me! Here are my personal 10 top tips for working from home:

1   Establish a routine. Don't let chaos reign. Try to work set hours with set breaks and don't give in to interruptions.

2   Don't allow the boundaries between your working life and your private life to become blurred. Keep the two as separate as you can.

3   Brush your teeth, have a shower, get dressed, etc in the morning before you start work, just as if you were going to a 'real' office. Get in the right frame of mind for work.

4   Try to work in a completely separate room – preferably one where you can close the door to (a) keep disturbances out and (b) keep the work in, and out of sight!

5   Avoid having a TV in the room where you work – and certainly avoid having the TV on whilst you work!

6   You may find work more enjoyable with music in the background but make sure you turn it off whenever you are on the telephone.

7   Recognise that you will be responsible for motivating yourself and maintaining self-discipline. Make a continual conscious effort in this respect.

8   Be aware that you might well suffer from feelings of loneliness and isolation. If this is the case then take positive steps to counteract this, such as seeing friends for lunch.

9   Make sure your friends and family (and maybe you too!) understand and appreciate that working from home means that you will actually be working. It's not a sort of semi day off!

10   Don't allow others to make you feel as if working from home doesn't constitute real work. Home workers often work pretty hard – and are generally highly productive.

Overcoming difficulties

Not everybody is actually suited to working from home because it does not allow face-to-face contact with colleagues on a daily basis. Whereas some will find that they are much more productive working by themselves, others may feel that the lack of direct contact with others within a supportive office environment hampers their progress. Therefore, people working from home require as much interaction with their manager as their office-based counterparts. It is important to establish effective management and support structures. Also, managers and employees alike may benefit from being given specific training to enhance their understanding of how to make remote working a success. Employees need to be trained in how best to manage their time effectively and managers need to be trained in the specific skills necessary for the management of remote workers.

It is argued that people working from home may lack the required motivation to enable them to complete their daily responsibilities and this, in turn, can result in their managers losing trust and confidence in them. Office-based colleagues have been known to harbour feelings of resentment towards remote workers and these are all issues that need to be handled very carefully. Remote workers still need to feel that they are valued members of the team and should therefore be given the same access to company information and team activities. This includes any available training courses that will enable them to have the same opportunities for advancement as their office-based colleagues.

The work allocated to remote workers should be appropriate in terms of it being suitable for completion away from the office but it should also be significant enough for the employee to feel that their role is of value to the organisation.

The environment in which a remote worker will be based should be assessed to ensure that it complies with health and safety legislation. Any work-related incidents that occur within a remote worker's home can actually be the responsibility of the organisation, so this is very important.

Managers are also responsible for ensuring that remote workers take regular breaks, including lunch, and that they do not feel tempted to work overly long hours. It can be easy to fall into the trap of working late into the evening simply because the work is always to hand.

Business travel

Remote working isn't, of course, just limited to those who work from home. Many people are required to travel on business – to visit clients and suppliers or to visit other branches of their organisation. Whilst travelling inevitably wastes a good deal of time, you can nevertheless try to use your time as productively as possible. If your new job requires you to travel on business for the first time – or even if you're an experienced business traveller – I have a few tips for you.

Wireless Internet connections (WiFi) are now commonplace and mean that work can even be done when on the move. If you travel on business then you'll most likely have a laptop. Make sure you know how to establish a WiFi connection with it so that you can catch up on e-mails, etc even when you're sitting waiting for a train.

You might also want to take a detailed report or a business book that you never normally seem to find the time to read through and use your travelling time (assuming you're not driving!) to study that in detail. Your time travelling could be one of the few occasions when you can spend a few hours without being interrupted by other people!

Even if you are driving, you could still use the time productively, for example by learning another language from a CD-based language course. If you regularly spend many hours on the road then that time will add up, and learning a new language should be perfectly feasible – and could significantly enhance your CV. As a salesman, my brother spends a significant proportion of his working life 'stuck' in his car – but has used what would otherwise be wasted time to become proficient in Spanish.

Working abroad

Your new job may even take you abroad, of course. You might consider this a significant perk, although travelling abroad on business (like all business travel) can often consist of a lot of work, a lot of waiting for trains and planes – and not much else! However, you could try to seize the opportunity to take a day or two off whilst you're out there and get some sightseeing done.

An important issue to take into account when travelling abroad is your health. Make sure you have appropriate health insurance or cover. If you are working for a UK employer but resident within the EEA (European Economic Area) for extended periods then you should apply to HMRC (Her Majesty's Revenue & Customs) so that you can receive health care abroad on the same basis as a local resident. And you should, of course, bear in mind necessary vaccinations and other medical treatments (for example anti-malaria) before you set off.

It's also worth taking the time to buy and read through a guide book to the country you're visiting. Guide books often contain plenty of useful practical information, such as local tipping practices, which will help your trip go much more smoothly.

Of course, your permanent place of work in your new job may well be outside the UK and that will be the subject of the next chapter.

Summary

- Compelling workers to work from their employer's premises is now a much less prevalent employer philosophy.

- Well over a million people in the UK work purely from home and nearly four million work largely from home.

- Not everybody is actually suited to working from home because it does not allow face-to-face contact with colleagues on a daily basis.

- Employees need to be trained in how best to manage their time effectively and managers need to be trained in the specific skills necessary for the management of remote workers.

- Remote workers still need to feel that they are valued members of the team and should therefore be given the same access to company information and team activities.

- Whilst travelling inevitably wastes a good deal of time, you can nevertheless try to use your time as productively as possible.

- If you regularly spend many hours on the road then that time will add up, and learning a new language should be perfectly feasible – and could significantly enhance your CV.

- An important issue to take into account when travelling abroad is your health. Make sure you have appropriate health insurance or cover.

18
Working abroad

Workplaces can vary quite considerably from country to country. However, whilst most of the basic principles remain similar, in this chapter I will discuss a few peculiarities of a selection of different countries which I know to be popular amongst my readers when it comes to living and working abroad.

Ireland (Éire)

Irish hospitality is famous, making it a very pleasant place to work. If you move to the Republic of Ireland (ROI) to start your new job then you should soon feel right at home, even though you might take time to get used to the accent!

Working in Ireland is very similar to working in the UK – more so than any other European country (and the UK is Ireland's largest trading partner). The pace of life might be slightly slower and more relaxed but that's probably a plus point – and there really aren't any negative ones.

English is the primary language with Irish only necessary for certain specific public sector jobs.

Whilst Ireland suffered a major economic downturn in the recession, it remains a vibrant and dynamic place in which to live and work. But jobs are scarce, so if you find yourself a job in Ireland, consider yourself lucky and celebrate with a Guinness or two!

France and Belgium

I should make it clear from the start that I personally live in France – and so my advice in this respect might not be entirely objective. I love France. However, working in France is a lot like eating Marmite. You either love it or you hate it!

Hundreds of thousands of Britons live in France. The food, the wine and the climate are all very appealing! Many foreigners in France are retired but there are also many who are working.

The first and most important thing to note about the French is the importance they attach to their language. English may be the international language of business – but not in France! Whilst a lot of your day-to-day work may very well involve English, it is vital that you make an effort to learn and to speak French. You're unlikely to get far without this; it's the very best way to integrate.

Learning French will help you to understand key cultural points such as whether to say *tu* to people ('you' singular, but also informal and used between family members, friends or colleagues) or *vous* ('you' plural, but also more formal). In English, we just say 'you' but in French, the distinction can be an important point of etiquette and getting it wrong can be insulting!

I could write a book about all the various cultural differences between the British and the French – and many people have already done so. I suggest you buy a few! The French can take time to get to understand but, once you do, you'll find they're a kind-hearted, decent and passionate people.

Workplaces are often more formal than in the UK but women should note that the boundaries on what constitutes sexual harassment are much more blurred in France than in the UK. What may constitute harassment in the UK may just be a normal, accepted – and expected – bit of harmless flirtation in France.

TOP TIP

In a foreign country, your gender won't necessarily be easy for the locals to deduce from your first name. Help them out in your written correspondence if necessary by stating clearly, in their own language, what your title is; for example, in France 'Mrs' becomes 'Mme'.

Germany, Austria and Switzerland

Germany is the largest national economy in Europe and one of the largest and most dynamic in the world, home to numerous world-famous multinationals. It is therefore a popular destination for many foreign workers.

Adapting to working in Germany can take some time, though. Their attitude to work is different from that in the UK. People don't tend to work long hours; they frequently leave work around 4 pm. However, there is great emphasis on efficiency. There's no time for chit-chat. Germans tend to knuckle down and work hard.

Punctuality is also very important. Germans don't appreciate lateness. As in France, workplaces are often more formal than in the UK.

Learning German isn't quite as important as learning French would be when living in France – but it's pretty important nonetheless! The ability to speak some degree of German will probably be a prerequisite of your working in Germany but, once there, do everything you can to improve your skills in this respect.

Italy

Italy is, of course, a very beautiful country and it is also an important European economic power.

Italians generally have a more relaxed approach to life than, say, Germans. They are friendly and welcoming to foreigners and always happy to help out if you're struggling with their language. And you certainly should be making an effort to learn their language. Whilst younger Italians may speak English well, the older generation often don't.

Whilst Germany may be a frighteningly efficient country, Italy is pretty much the opposite. Italian bureaucracy is legendary; everything takes far more time and is far more complicated than it should be. The answer is to accept this as a fact of life; the Italians do! You need to adapt to their way of life.

Personal contacts and networking are of great importance in Italy. If you are to fit in successfully you need to integrate, get to know people, make friends and build up a network of useful contacts – including other expatriates. You'll soon find out that your social network is a very valuable resource – in both your professional and your personal lives.

Spain

Despite significant economic problems, the quality of life in Spain is very high – quite possibly because work takes second place and family and social life comes first! The boundaries between the two are often blurred. Business deals are often concluded over casual and lengthy lunches (due to the heat, Spaniards tend to take very long lunch breaks and then work into the early evening).

Like the Italians, the Spanish are known for their bureaucracy. You just have to take that as part and parcel of living and working there. You'll also have to adjust to such traditions as *mañana*, meaning 'tomorrow'. As the old Spanish proverb goes, 'Tomorrow is often the busiest day of the week.' This is on account of the fact that if you ask someone to get something done and ask them when they'll do it, they'll invariably reply '*Mañana*'! Another favourite expression is '*No problema*' ('No problem').

But you'll soon learn not to take either of these expressions literally! *Mañana*, for example, generally means anything but tomorrow! But this is perhaps also why the incidence of stress-related illness is much lower in Spain.

Whilst moving to live and work in Spain can be quite a culture shock, if you make an effort to adapt you'll find it a very rewarding country – and the Spanish a generous and charming people.

United States of America

More people want to live and work in the USA than in any other country – which is perhaps why it's so difficult to get to live and work there. Unless you're married to an American (and even then it's not easy) you have to be 'sponsored' by your employer to get a work visa.

The USA has a lot to be said for it. It has by far the greatest GDP (gross domestic product) of any country in the world – on a par with that of the entire European Union put together! New York, Chicago and Los Angeles are amongst the most economically powerful cities in the world and the state of California alone is one of the world's top 10 largest economies. Despite the credit crunch, pay levels remain relatively high and the cost of living remains relatively low.

For natives of the UK and Ireland, it is a home from home – almost. As Oscar Wilde said, 'We have really everything in common with America nowadays except, of course, language.' But I've already covered some of the differences between British English and American English back in Chapter 14, Writing skills. They're really very minor and you'll soon get used to them.

Canada

If you've never been to Canada, you may be forgiven for thinking it's an icy cold country where bears roam the streets. Whilst there is a small element of truth in this, you need to bear in mind that 90 per cent of Canada's population lives within 100 miles of the US border, enjoying a climate very similar to that in the UK. (OK; I accept that the British climate may not be the best in the world either!)

Canada is, of course, a country of two languages – English and French – with English-speaking regions and French-speaking regions. That said, you will be able to get along in English pretty well, right the way across the country.

With a rich history, Toronto, the capital, is a cultural mosaic and a major economic centre – one of the top 10 most economically powerful cities in the world. It's also largely English speaking.

What is it actually like working with Canadians? Working life is said to be more laid back and less stressful than in the UK but, to be honest, there aren't many countries where it isn't! And the overall quality of living is very high.

Australia and New Zealand

Australia and New Zealand are amongst the most popular destinations in the world for international visitors. The lifestyle and stunning landscapes and climate are all compelling draws – as is the low population density.

Most people should have no difficulties settling Down Under, just so long as they know what to expect. The working environment is not dissimilar to the UK's although, as in so many other countries, it's more relaxed, far less structured and more informal. Don't expect to see much in the way of suits and ties. Working hours are lower and many people finish pretty early on a Friday. POETS day is a popular national institution!

The Middle East

The Middle East is a broad geographical region, comprising at least 18 different countries and, economically, best known for the production of oil. However, it is also an important centre for construction, engineering, finance, IT and other industries.

In the 1980s, the UAE began establishing economic 'free zones' (tax-free areas), making the country highly attractive to foreign professionals who, in some places (such as Dubai), outnumber the locals!

There is a very strong work ethic with most people putting in very long hours but there is also a strong and vibrant expatriate community offering all sorts of possibilities for you to spend your hard-earned money living it up!

Despite popular opinion to the contrary, most areas in the Middle East are safe and welcoming for foreigners – and English is spoken just about everywhere.

South Africa

South Africa enjoys the most advanced economy in Africa. However, although apartheid officially ended in 1991, it is still a country with significant divisions. As it is one of the most ethnically diverse countries in the world, numerous different languages are spoken. However, English is very widely understood and commonly used in business.

South America

South America obviously covers quite a number of different countries (a dozen, to be precise) and they're all a little different – but they also have a lot of common ground.

You will generally find working life reasonably casual – certainly when it comes to dress codes and working hours. You will also find that great importance is attached to personal contacts and networking – very similar to Spain and Italy.

Every country is slightly different, of course, and it pays to do some research before you get out there. Any organisation that hires a person in Argentina, for example, will send them for a medical and psychological exam called *examen preocupacional*. This is undertaken by clinics specialising in *medicina laboral* (occupational medicine) and its purpose is to identify pre-existing medical conditions and so protect the employer against claims that medical conditions were caused by their work. The mental health element aims to identify conditions such as OCD, psychosis, klepto-mania, pyromaniac, etc and so can be quite intimidating!

Summary

- Workplaces can vary quite considerably from country to country.

- Irish hospitality is famous and you should soon feel right at home, even though you might take time to get used to the accent!

- In a foreign country, your gender won't necessarily be easy for the locals to deduce from your first name.

- Help them out in your written correspondence if necessary by stating clearly, in their own language, what your title is; for example, in France 'Mrs' becomes 'Mme'.

- The first and most important thing to note about the French is the importance they attach to their language.

- In Germany, there is great emphasis on efficiency. There's no time for chit-chat. Germans tend to knuckle down and work hard. Punctuality is also very important.

- Italian bureaucracy is legendary; everything takes far more time and is far more complicated than it should be. The answer is to accept this as a fact of life.

- Despite significant economic problems, the quality of life in Spain is very high – quite possibly because work takes second place and family and social life comes first!

- For natives of the UK and Ireland, the USA is a home from home. Any language differences are really very minor and you'll soon get used to them.

- Canada is a country of two languages – English and French. That said, you will be able to get along in English pretty well, right the way across the country.

- Down Under, working hours are lower and many people finish pretty early on a Friday. POETS day is a popular national institution!

- Despite popular opinion to the contrary, most areas in the Middle East are safe and welcoming for foreigners – and English is spoken just about everywhere.

PART FIVE
COPING WITH PROBLEMS

19

Dealing with difficult people

Nobody said starting a new job was easy. If it was, then whole books wouldn't have been written to help people through the ordeal! There will inevitably be problems to deal with and overcome and, in the next few chapters, I'll therefore be covering some of these problems.

Unfortunately, the most common source of problems in a new job is other people – difficult people. And how you handle difficult people will demonstrate pretty much everything anyone needs to know about your interpersonal skills.

When it comes to dealing with interpersonal conflict, there are three main ways in which you might react:

- Do you clash head-on with difficult people?

- Do you run away and hide?!

- Do you find ways to deal with them?

Which of these three categories do you fall into?

You do, of course, want to fall firmly into the third category. You want to demonstrate to your new boss and to your new colleagues that you are someone who, when faced with a difficult colleague (or customer, for that matter) will find ways to deal with them – and to put your relationship on a more positive footing. It's a great opportunity to portray yourself as a true professional.

Nobody wants a hothead who is just going to clash with their colleagues, nor do they want someone who is going to be prone to being bullied. Most working environments contain at least one 'difficult' person – it's the school bully syndrome. And you're most likely already fully aware of just who that person is or who those people are in your new job. Difficult people are a fact of life and you've got to show that you can cope with them – not only that you can cope with them but that you can, in spite of the difficulties, successfully work with such individuals.

Whilst it might seem blatantly obvious what makes someone difficult to work with, everyone has a different perception of what makes a colleague difficult. And research has shown there to be a number of different, specific personality types which are likely to cause problems in the workplace.

Assertiveness

When it comes to dealing with difficult people, empathy is very important but it's vital to be assertive with it or you're not going to get very far.

In the majority of working environments, there are people who are naturally dominant and those who are more submissive. Generally, the difference between these two types of people is their level of self-confidence. However, there are proven ways to increase self-confidence and, therefore, the ability to assert oneself.

Being assertive can be defined in a number of ways, including the ability to resist the dominant behaviour of others. Those lacking in assertiveness often find themselves doing things simply to please other people and agreeing with others just to keep the peace. They may continually allow people to criticise them and, as a result, feel inferior to others. Many workplaces have at least one person who is considered to be a bully and the more you are able to assert yourself the better equipped you will be to stand up to them – particularly in the first few days and weeks of your new relationship. Assertiveness also enables you to gain more control over challenging situations.

Assertiveness can often be a particular problem for women. Assertive behaviour – or even aggressive behaviour – coming from a man is still often seen as socially acceptable. However, coming from a woman, it's often seen as less socially acceptable. Ignore the social conventions; we're all equal and women need to be just as assertive in the workplace as men, if not more so if they're to counter old-fashioned social prejudices.

Being assertive should not, however, be confused with being aggressive. Assertive behaviour is not hostile behaviour. There's no attacking, threatening or blaming involved. It simply involves standing up for yourself and not letting yourself be pushed around and abused. The key difference is that you're standing up for what is rightfully yours, not trespassing on the rights of others with impunity. Being assertive doesn't mean being a bully!

Team player or bully?

There is a clear difference between a good team player and a bully. A good team player encourages development within the team and involves others in decision making and group activities, whereas a bully tends to threaten others into delivering what they want and fails to recognise the strengths and achievements of others. Their dominance is usually rewarded by results which they perceive as a reinforcement of their behaviour. Their ability to control others often enables them to acquire a network of 'supporters' who are, to all intents and purposes, at their beck and call. However, take the bully away from their loyal allies and they are not always as tough as they first appear to be.

Coping with bullies

When faced with a confrontation involving a dominant person or a bully, there are ways to improve your ability to cope with the situation.

First, it is important to know your aggressor and their behaviour so that you can anticipate what is likely to happen and therefore prepare accordingly. Knowing that you are well prepared should be an immediate boost to your self-confidence.

Next, you should be equipped with all the facts necessary to enable you to make your case. This level of organisation will help you to respond to any questions you are faced with and allow you to defend yourself should the need arise. Ask probing questions that will require the other person to explain their position in detail. Often, dominant people will be relying on their bullying tactics to win the confrontation and will therefore not have prepared as well as you have. This will give you an immediate advantage over them.

Here are five key pointers to help you to deal with bullies:

1 Don't let them see that they're getting to you. If they see they're getting a reaction it's more than likely to encourage them to bully further. Don't play their game.

2 Don't give them any excuses. Perform to the best of your ability and don't leave yourself open to criticism.

3 Don't let them make you feel that you're at fault in any way. That's just playing into their hands.

4 Don't expect that you are going to be able to change the bully's behaviour. Only they can really change their own behaviour.

5 If bullying becomes a serious problem then start documenting incidents with a view to making a formal complaint if it becomes necessary.

Keep calm and believe in yourself

The more you allow a bully to dominate, the more they will continue to do so. Allow yourself time before answering to ensure that your responses are what you want to say rather than what they want you to say. Do not allow yourself to show fear and try not to react to their bullying tactics. Play to your own strengths and use your own particular style to defend your position.

Be nice to bullies!

Strange as it may seem, bullies do actually deserve your sympathy. Their behaviour is often the result of their own insecurities and can be rooted in their childhood experiences. Often, they have been victims themselves in the past and are using their aggressive behaviour to help restore their own confidence. If you show sympathy to a bully, they will automatically be at a psychological disadvantage as they come to realise that their dominant behaviour has failed to control you.

Sexual harassment

Before moving on to ways in which you can develop your assertiveness, I'd just like to say a few words about harassment – and sexual harassment in particular. There's a fine line between when someone's aggressive behaviour becomes bullying and a very fine line thereafter before it becomes harassment. And by far the most troubling form of harassment in the workplace is sexual harassment. Sexual harassment is bullying, intimidation or coercion of a sexual nature – or the attempted control and manipulation of others in exchange for sexual favours. There's a whole spectrum of sexual harassment from mild harassment, which you might construe as harmless, through to sexual harassment, which is downright illegal. Sexual harassment is legally considered to be a form of discrimination.

When faced with sexual harassment, you might feel the situation is one of a simple misunderstanding. The harasser may not even be aware their behaviour is a problem – or illegal. Your first step should be, in most cases, to try to take the issue up with the person causing the problem – either face to face or, if you prefer, in writing – but, failing that, don't hesitate to go over their head to a higher authority. Most employers take the issue of sexual harassment very seriously indeed – and, left 'untreated', it's normally a problem which will just grow and grow with time. Nip it in the bud before things go too far.

But before making a formal complaint, do be careful to document incidents in detail, including, if possible, details of witnesses. You need proof.

It's also worth noting that it's not just women who can become victims of sexual harassment. Young men with powerful female bosses can also find themselves facing such difficulties. Not all harassers are even of the opposite gender. The common factor is usually one person being in a position of power over another – and abusing that position of power for their own sexual benefit.

Developing assertiveness

You can learn to be more assertive, although this does come more naturally to some people than to others. There are, of course, training courses and workshops available at many colleges and education centres that are designed to help you to practise assertiveness but here are my own top 10 key tips in this respect:

1 Don't be unreasonably afraid of displeasing others; if you're not being aggressive then this shouldn't be an issue.

2 Don't feel that you should have to be liked by everyone; being assertive shouldn't mean that you are disliked but the fear of being disliked can inhibit your ability to assert yourself.

3 Don't let your tone of voice rise at the end of a statement so as to make it sound like a question, communicating to the listener that you have doubts about what you're saying.

4 Don't allow yourself to express unnecessary doubts about what you're saying (eg 'I may be wrong, but...').

5 Don't apologise unnecessarily (eg 'I'm sorry, but I disagree.'). You should only be apologising if you're at fault. There's no shame in disagreeing.

6 Don't let yourself feel under attack if somebody else disagrees with you. In the workplace, it's rarely personal. It's just business.

7 Don't be afraid of saying no when necessary and appropriate. It's one of the most powerful words in the English language!

8 Don't let people cut you off in the middle of what you're saying. Ask them politely to hear you out.

9 Do stand up straight and maintain eye contact when talking to someone – and gently resting your hand on their arm can also be useful in getting them to take notice of you.

10 Don't be discouraged if you feel you handled an exchange less assertively than you should have done; recognise your failing and resolve to do better next time round.

However you work to develop and enhance your assertiveness, be prepared for the changes you will see in yourself. Those around you may feel uncomfortable with the person you become, but the people that know you best will very soon adapt to the new, more confident you. By becoming more assertive, you should find that you are able to express your needs and emotions in a much clearer and more concise way and, as a result, be much happier in the workplace.

Dealing with difficult bosses

A difficult new boss is always a challenge – but not an impossible one. You first need to try to understand why they're difficult – or why you perceive them to be difficult. Is it pressure and stress? Is it just their personal character? Is it simply a lack of management skills?

Once you've got a better understanding of the difficulties, you need to manage your own negative reactions to this behaviour. Don't let it cause you to be stressed or otherwise engage in counterproductive and self-defeating behaviour. Rise above it!

Dealing with a difficult boss isn't really that different from dealing with any other difficult person; it's just that you have a greater need to deal with them effectively! You should find that reading back through some of the ideas and techniques in Chapter 7, Managing your new boss, should be very helpful in making your boss a little less difficult to cope with.

How assertive are you?

Work your way through the following 10 questions to see how assertive you really are and whether it's an area you need to tackle. For each question, score 1 for 'Very unlikely', 2 for 'Not likely', 3 for 'Likely', 4 for 'Very likely', and 5 for 'Definitely':

1 If your opinion differs from that of the person you're talking to, how likely are you to express it?

2 If someone queue-barges are you likely to complain?

3 At a conference, how likely are you to mix and mingle and meet new people?

4 If a salesperson persists in trying to sell you something, how likely are you to tell them to leave you alone?

5 Are you likely to open your mouth and fight your corner in an argument?

6 If someone is causing you problems, are you likely to confront them about it and try to find a solution?

7 If you're working with a colleague and their contribution is substandard, are you likely to take it up with them?

8 If you're talking to someone and they're clearly misinformed, are you likely to set them straight?

9 If you need someone's help, how likely are you to actually ask for it?

10 If someone tries to force additional work on you which you really can't manage, how likely are you to refuse?

Add up your scores. If you scored under 25 then being sufficiently assertive could well be a problem for you. If you scored under 15 then it's definitely a problem and you need to find solutions to help you to develop your assertiveness. If you answered 'Very unlikely' to any of the questions then re-read that question and think through in your own mind how you might be able to change that behaviour pattern in future.

Asserting yourself in a new job isn't always easy. Being the 'new kid on the block' can put you at an immediate disadvantage. But the ball's very much in your court to redress the balance and not let yourself be pushed around by others. Don't run away and hide!

Summary

- How you handle difficult people will demonstrate pretty much everything anyone needs to know about your interpersonal skills.

- Do you clash head-on with difficult people? Do you run away and hide?! Or do you find ways to deal with them?

- You want to demonstrate that you are someone who, when faced with a difficult colleague, will find ways to deal with them – and to put your relationship on a more positive footing.

- Nobody wants a hothead who is just going to clash with their colleagues, nor do they want someone who is going to be prone to being bullied.

- Empathy is very important but it's vital to be assertive with it or you're not going to get very far.

- Being assertive can be defined in a number of ways, including the ability to resist the dominant behaviour of others.

- Many workplaces have at least one person who is considered to be a bully, and the more you are able to assert yourself the better equipped you will be to stand up to them.

- The more you allow a bully to dominate, the more they will continue to do so.

- If you show sympathy to a bully, they will automatically be at a psychological disadvantage as they come to realise that their dominant behaviour has failed to control you.

20
Handling office politics

The advice here is really very simple: Avoid getting negatively caught up in gossip, office politics and horseplay right from the start!

That's not to say that you won't suffer from it, though...

Is it our qualifications that help us to move up the career ladder? Is it our experience? No, it's other people! Whether we like it or not, the people we work with have a much greater influence on how far our careers progress than do our actual talents or work ethic.

The harsh reality

Many people think their workplaces are devoid of office politics; they're generally not. And it's normally those who are the most politically savvy who manage to make their way to the top fastest.

That doesn't mean you need to indulge in office politics, though. Being politically savvy is not the same as being politically aggressive. Yes, you need to seek to understand the new people you now work with – and what their professional agendas are. But not so that you can then engage them in battle. You need to understand them because, once you do, you'll have a much better chance of being able to handle them – and of being understood yourself. Don't make the mistake of thinking that all those engaged in office politics are doing so with the aim of furthering their own careers; some are stupid enough to make matters personal and to have specific targeted individuals in the workplace whom they are trying to disparage just for the sake of it. Steer well clear of this!

As our world becomes ever more competitive, understanding the political landscape of an organisation has never been more important. And, whilst you should try to act with decency and integrity, you definitely shouldn't expect that everyone else will be doing the same.

Dirty tricks campaigns

Office politics can extend from elementary jockeying for position through to down-right dirty tricks.

Atari founder Nolan Bushnell said, 'Business is a good game – lots of competition and a minimum of rules. You keep score with money.' The same could be said of office politics. Here are some common nasty little tricks which might be played on you by a 'colleague':

- publicly supporting you/your project whilst simultaneously plotting your/its downfall;

- taking disproportionate amounts of credit for your work – or quite simply stealing your ideas and taking all the credit;

- hiding their own opinion by talking around a subject in an effort to get you to fully disclose your own opinion first – and then using that against you;

- deliberately withholding important, relevant information so that you make a wrong decision, even though it may have been the best decision given the information available;

- leaving you off an e-mail distribution list or a meeting agenda so that you miss out on vital information.

How are you to react in the face of such underhandedness? Well, don't let it get personal and, where different factions are involved, don't take sides. Stay on the fence. Stay neutral. There's a lot to be said for neutrality – just look at how successful a policy it's been for Switzerland!

Aggressive office politicians may rise high but the top posts are normally won by those who have the greatest all-round appeal.

Win–win situations

Try to make all your interactions win–win situations. Political conflicts are the result of conflicting interests. Everyone wants to be a winner – and most people think that for them to win, someone else has to lose. In the workplace, that doesn't have to be the case.

Aggressive office politicians will usually try to engineer win–lose situations – but that's not a good long-term recipe for winning friends and influencing people. That's their weakness – and they rarely realise it. If you strive to achieve win–win situations then it's not only in your employer's best interests but it's also in your own best interests from a political point of view. It's an enduring strategy that will stand you in good stead in the long term.

Gossip

Office gossip is closely related to office politics. Those who engage in office politics clearly do so with the objective of gaining an advantage. Gossips, on the other hand, may just be gossiping for the sake of it. And it's a very nasty habit. You will, however, find that most gossips also have a political agenda and gossip is just one of an arsenal of tools they use to help them to manipulate the thoughts, feelings and opinions of others. Manipulation is at the very heart (and a cold, cold heart it can be) of office politics. And, as Philip K. Dick said, 'The basic tool for the manipulation of reality is the manipulation of words.'

It's a dangerous game – and I'd recommend you avoid playing it at all in your new job. Everyone knows a gossip but does anyone ever have a particularly high opinion of them? Gossips often feel they're a real hub of the workplace – at the centre of all the action – and it's this kind of buzz that inspires and feeds their behaviour. But what they neglect is that, no matter how riveting what they have to say might be, most people find gossiping pretty distasteful and, by extension, are likely to find the gossip themselves pretty distasteful too. After all, just imagine what they might be saying behind your own back!

In your new job, you will want to pay attention to the grapevine – but avoid contributing to it. Your new colleagues will be watching you closely during your first few days, weeks and months in your new job and you definitely don't want to develop a reputation as a gossipmonger.

At the end of the day, many workplaces are like playgrounds – watch out for the bullies and the telltales, don't get involved in gangs – and certainly don't let anyone take your lunch money!

Here are some top tips to help prevent you from becoming embroiled in office gossip:

- Limit your association with office gossips. Simple as that. Steer subtly clear of them if at all possible.

- If you're confronted with gossip then use your initiative to simply change the subject. Stop gossip dead in its tracks by talking about something else.

- If you're in a group and they start gossiping then find a good excuse to get up and leave. Don't participate.

- Let gossip die when it reaches you. Don't even think about passing it on, however great the temptation. Passing it on just throws fuel on the flames.

- Never gossip yourself. Lead by example. When you choose not to gossip, you send a clear message that it's something you're not prepared to tolerate.

Summary

- Avoid getting negatively caught up in gossip, office politics and horseplay right from the start!

- Whether we like it or not, the people we work with have a much greater influence on how far our careers progress than do our actual talents or work ethic.

- Many people think their workplaces are devoid of office politics; they're generally not.

- It's normally those who are the most politically savvy who manage to make their way to the top fastest.

- That doesn't mean you need to indulge in office politics, though. Being politically savvy is not the same as being politically aggressive.

- Whilst you should try to act with decency and integrity, you definitely shouldn't expect that everyone else will be doing the same.

- Office politics can extend from elementary jockeying for position through to downright dirty tricks.

- Don't let it get personal and, where different factions are involved, don't take sides. Stay on the fence. Stay neutral.

- Aggressive office politicians may rise high but the top posts are normally won by those who have the greatest all-round appeal.

- Try to make all your interactions win–win situations. It's an enduring strategy that will stand you in good stead in the long term.

21
Pressure and stress

The ability to cope with pressure and stress is essential in almost all walks of life, whether you're working checkout at the supermarket or heading up a major corporation. Pressure and stress are unavoidable aspects of the world we live in and it's important to give these issues serious consideration when starting out in a new job.

The difference between pressure and stress

Do you fully understand what the difference is between pressure and stress? Many people use the two terms interchangeably.

Being under pressure is a matter of having significant demands made of you – being challenged to achieve something which is either difficult to achieve in and of itself or difficult to achieve within the time frame that has been set. Pressure is largely a positive force and a motivating factor for many people.

Stress, on the other hand, is not so positive. Stress occurs when the pressure you are under exceeds your ability to effectively meet the demands being made of you. Stress is essentially what an individual experiences when exposed to excessive pressure – and long-term stress can cause all sorts of problems.

I am sure that everyone reading this book will, at some stage in their lives, have experienced pressure and stress and know exactly what they're like – and you'll be particularly at risk of stress when starting a new job.

Stress in the workplace

In recent times, stress has increasingly become one of the most common causes of absence from work, often leading to long-term absence or even resignation. Many employers are becoming aware of the importance of the well-being of their staff to maintaining productivity levels and are therefore introducing specific policies to ensure the effective management of stress in the workplace.

There are a number of factors recognised as being triggers of stress and stress-related illnesses and these can be found both at home and in the workplace. The symptoms vary dramatically from person to person and can be relatively minor or, at the other end of the spectrum, can be very severely debilitating. The key is stress prevention and there are many effective techniques that both an individual and their employer can use to prevent, reduce and manage stress within the workplace.

The causes of pressure and stress

Different people respond in different ways to the challenges that arise in the workplace and what is a major stress factor for some may be a simple problem easily overcome by others. It is important to remember that it is not a sign of weakness to feel the effects of stress more than your colleagues do and, perhaps ironically, making comparisons between yourself and your peers can actually increase stress levels further still!

Most jobs involve some unavoidable pressures and demands that can cause feelings of stress. A certain level of pressure can be seen as positive because it can improve motivation, performance and job satisfaction whilst also providing you with an overall sense of achievement. However, excessive stress is particularly damaging. Positive pressure can result from an effective manager setting high standards and reasonable targets to facilitate their achievement. It can also be the result of productive working relationships with colleagues. Negative stress factors are numerous and include the following:

- conflicting demands;
- job insecurity;
- confusion over job responsibilities;
- inflexible timetable;
- working long or unsociable hours;
- conflict with other individuals;
- feeling undervalued or unappreciated;
- lack of management support;

- poor working conditions;

- changing management infrastructure;

- unreasonable workload;

- bullying or harassment;

- unfair treatment;

- working in isolation;

- reduced responsibility.

The effects of stress

The effects of stress can appear as either mental or physical symptoms with varying degrees of severity. Some of the many physical symptoms include:

- insomnia;

- excessive tiredness;

- being overly emotional;

- panic attacks;

- headaches;

- change in dietary habits;

- digestive problems.

The most common mental symptoms include:

- irritability;

- apathy;

- loss of concentration;

- withdrawal;

- anxiety;

- mood swings;

- suppressed anger.

Now that employers are more aware of the seriousness of stress and stress-related illnesses, many organisations are adopting a more proactive approach to combating the causes of stress. By identifying the symptoms of stress as early as possible, the more serious symptoms, ie those leading to long periods of time off work, can be avoided. By reviewing existing policies, management and communication systems, and by implementing subsequent improvements, an employer can effectively remove many of the stress triggers.

Combating stress

If you do start to recognise the symptoms of stress, there are a number of ways which can help to prevent it becoming more serious. It is particularly helpful if you are able to identify your own particular stress triggers so that you can then take positive steps towards dealing with them effectively. There are specific lifestyle changes you can make that are believed to reduce stress levels and these include:

- taking regular exercise;
- maintaining a healthy, balanced diet;
- reducing alcohol consumption;
- stopping smoking (in the long term!);
- practising yoga, meditation, etc.

In the workplace, it is also possible to organise your day in such a way as to reduce the impact of stress triggers. We talked in detail about time management techniques in Chapter 12. If possible, prepare a list of your daily responsibilities and arrange this in order of priority. Tackle the most challenging tasks first and the sense of achievement you experience upon their completion should make handling the rest of your work much easier.

However, if you feel bogged down, with too much work outstanding, try to delegate if possible. There is no shame in asking for help – your manager is more likely to prefer a job to be done well than for it to have been rushed.

Stress is now recognised as a particularly serious illness with symptoms that are often difficult to manage. It is essential to seek professional help from a doctor, counsellor or even from your personnel manager if the symptoms you experience are becoming more serious. It is also important to remember that your manager may be just as concerned about your health and well-being as you are and, if you communicate your concerns to them, you will probably find that they will go out of their way to help you.

Work–life balance

There's an old joke that when it comes to addressing your work–life balance you first need to review your list of priorities:

- family;

- job;

- exercise;

- holidays;

- must-dos;

- medical;

- eating;

- hygiene;

- sleep;

- romance.

But the catch is that you only have time for three things – work and holidays are two – and you get to pick a third!

There is no doubt that the 21st century is one that is seeing significantly increasing levels of consumer demand – with the need for services to be provided all day, every day. Understandably, this increase in demand is putting enormous pressure on the service providers themselves, leading to individuals working longer and more antisocial hours. As a result, many people have found themselves spending more time at the office and much less time at home.

Traditionally, it has been working mothers who are most associated with the need to achieve a work–life balance to enable them to spend quality time with their children whilst also allowing them to continue to bring in a wage. However, in these modern times, where equal rights are at the forefront of employment legislation, it is no longer just mothers who are entitled to a more flexible working day. Fathers are now being given the right to take paid paternity leave and many people are offered flexible hours to enable them to continue acting as carers for other members of their family. As mentioned in Chapter 17, in 2002 the UK government passed the Employment Act, stating that any employee with children under the age of six should have the right to request flexible working hours and that all employers should be obliged to give such requests serious consideration. Also, people with no dependents need to achieve an appropriate work–life balance to enable them to continue their training, to travel or simply to enjoy more time pursuing leisure activities.

There are undeniable advantages to employers who offer flexible working hours to their staff. They can enable them to provide a round-the-clock service to their customers and can also increase productivity as a result of the improved levels of motivation within the workforce. Absenteeism can be reduced and employee retention levels improved. Also, an employer that is seen to promote flexible working can be a popular choice for prospective jobseekers.

Even if your employer does not currently support flexible working practices, it is possible to make certain changes that will enable you to improve your quality of life. Limit the number of days you stay late at the office, allow yourself time off to attend family activities whenever possible and take regular breaks to ensure that you do not work for long periods at a time.

A healthy work–life balance is essential to helping you to cope with the inevitable stresses and strains of your working life.

What's your work–life balance like?

Once you've been in your new job for a good few months, spend a few minutes to take the following quiz and you should soon get a pretty clear idea as to whether you've got your work–life balance under control – or whether it's spiralling out of control!

Score 1 for 'Definitely not', 2 for 'Not really', 3 for 'True', 4 for 'Very true', and 5 for 'Too true':

1 I find I have far too little time free for my friends and family.

2 It troubles me that my family and friends generally think of me as a workaholic.

3 It's like I have to sacrifice myself daily for the sake of my work.

4 My husband/wife/partner/children seem to think I'm married to my job.

5 There are so many things I would like to do but don't have the energy for.

6 I have constant regrets about what I'm unable to find the time to do.

7 I feel too much of my life is wasted doing things I have to do, not things I want to do.

8 I lie in bed thinking about work, sleep badly and often dream I'm working/at work.

9 I find it hard to relax and just do nothing, even when I'm away on holiday.

10 I don't have enough time to exercise, eat properly and keep myself healthy.

11 Every minute of every day is always taken up with something; there's no spare time.

12 I can't remember the last time I just 'wasted' an entire day doing nothing but relaxing.

13 I feel burnt out, exhausted and unable to give my all to any area of my life.

14 My house/paperwork/car/dog is a mess! I just can't keep on top of everything.

15 I pin a lot of hope on winning the lottery/inheriting a fortune/retiring so I can just be free.

Add up your scores. If you scored over 25 then your work–life balance definitely needs some work. If you scored over 50 then serious action is required immediately. If you answered 'Too true' to any of the questions then there's definitely a major problem and you need to think long and hard about what changes you can make to your work–life balance so as to get it on a much more even keel.

Starting a new job will inevitably destabilise your work–life balance but you must make sure that it's only short term. It's not surprising that your new job will put you under more stress, strain and pressure but this should only be for the first few months. If, after six months, your work–life balance is still a mess then take action – immediately!

Summary

- The ability to cope with pressure and stress is essential in almost all walks of life, whether you're working checkout at the supermarket or heading up a major corporation.

- Being under pressure is a matter of having significant demands made of you.

- Stress occurs when the pressure you are under exceeds your ability to effectively meet the demands being made of you.

- The symptoms range dramatically from person to person and can be relatively minor or, at the other end of the spectrum, can be very severely debilitating.

- The key is stress prevention and there are many effective techniques that both an individual and their employer can use to prevent, reduce and manage stress within the workplace.

- The effects of stress can lead to a wide variety of mental and physical symptoms with varying degrees of severity, including insomnia, excessive tiredness and loss of concentration.

- By identifying the symptoms of stress as early as possible, the more serious symptoms, ie those leading to long periods of time off work, can be avoided.

- It is particularly helpful if you are able to identify your own particular stress triggers so that you can then take positive steps towards dealing with them effectively.

- It is essential to seek professional help from a doctor, counsellor or even from your personnel manager if the symptoms you experience are becoming more serious.

- A healthy work–life balance is essential to helping you to cope with the inevitable stresses and strains of your working life.

22

Coping with change at work

Change in the workplace is inevitable for a variety of often essential and unavoidable reasons. However, unless change is managed effectively – by both employer and employees – it can have a very negative impact – on both employer and employees.

Change is never easy. The majority of us instinctively want things to remain the way they are. Better the devil you know!

But there's no avoiding change, so you might as well learn not only how to cope with it but how to thrive on it. In this chapter we'll deal with how to deal with having change imposed on you. In the next chapter, we'll discuss imposing change from a management point of view.

The reasons for change

Some of the most common reasons for workplace change include:

- technological developments;

- process or procedural improvements;

- market or economic developments;

- merger or acquisition;

- corporate restructuring;

- increasing consumer demand.

What will be the impact?

The way people react to change is a lot like the way people react to bereavement; it's natural – you're experiencing a loss. Just as you've got yourself settled into your new job, it's as if someone has pulled the rug out from under your feet. You can therefore expect to go through a range of different emotions – from shock and denial to guilt, bargaining, anger and, finally, acceptance. The quicker you get yourself past the initial shock and on to the stage of accepting the change and moving on, the better.

The importance of communication

It is very likely that you will not be the only one to be affected by the changing circumstances, so it is important to maintain strong relationships with your peers. This enables you to share information with each other and also to provide mutual support.

As I made clear in Chapter 13, communication is always important – but it's even more so when you're confronted by significant changes.

On a purely practical basis, you do, of course, need to communicate clearly with those who are imposing the changes (normally your boss) so that you understand what is happening and what is expected of you.

Beyond the people you currently work with, reach out to your network and get advice from them, gaining from the benefit of their experience. That's what they're there for.

Seize the opportunities

Workplace change does not have to create stress and confusion. If you embrace the new ways of working, it can instead be an opportunity to acquire new skills and ultimately achieve career progression. As long as you remain flexible and responsive, you should be able to adapt to the new situation and ensure that you make the most of any new opportunities that are presented to you. The more you can see change as a positive and progressive issue, the better you'll be able to cope with it and to identify and seize the opportunities change brings.

Yes, change can be disruptive and disconcerting. There's absolutely no doubt about that. The status quo is almost always more comfortable – and we humans are naturally reticent about stepping outside our comfort zones. This is why it is important to remain calm and to maintain a positive attitude to change. See change as a positive influence; find the opportunities it brings with it; embrace it. It's good news!

For one thing, it's an excellent opportunity to impress your boss; your boss will most likely be having a tough time implementing the changes and they need all the support they can get! It's also an excellent opportunity to get yourself noticed, respected – and maybe even admired – by your colleagues for your ability to not only survive the changes but to thrive on them.

Training can be very useful in helping you to cope with change. Undertake any necessary or available training to ensure you are able to respond effectively. For example, if the change involves the introduction of new technology, take the opportunity to get thoroughly to grips with it. It's an ideal opportunity to put a business case to the management in support of your undertaking further training – at their expense! We'll cover the importance of ongoing training in further detail in Chapter 25, Training.

You may even wish to consider techniques such as NLP (Neuro-linguistic programming). What is NLP? It's the practice of understanding how you organise your thinking, feeling, language and behaviour to achieve results. It's a popular psychotherapy technique and often applied to organisational change. Whilst it has many critics, and the scientific evidence in favour of it is currently thin, it does also have numerous proponents and many people swear by it. Feel free to give it a go. Nothing ventured; nothing gained! I'd love to hear about your experiences with NLP.

How to cope on a personal and daily basis

I can boil down my key advice on coping with change at work to the following five tips:

1 Recognise and accept that change is inevitable. Your job is to rise to the challenge and to make the most of the opportunities it brings with it. Be willing to change.

2 Make sure you fully understand the reasons for the changes being made. It'll make them a whole lot easier to accept.

3 Maintain a positive attitude despite the uncertainties you may be facing. Keep giving 100 per cent to your work. When the going gets tough, the tough get going!

4 Link up with other positive people and stay away from the complainers. Don't let their negativity and resistance to change take you down with them.

5 Accept that there are going to be some difficult times. Learn to tolerate the discomfort. Remember that it's only temporary. Everything changes; nothing stays the same!

Keep the big picture in view

We've previously discussed the importance of understanding where you and your role fit into the bigger picture – what exactly your purpose is within your team, within your department and within the organisation as a whole. That big picture is now changing; it's evolving.

If your role is changing then you need to understand how those changes relate to the overall aims and objectives of the organisation and what specific contributions your team is expected to make in this respect.

This will help you to more fully understand the decisions made by the management.

Don't let it get you down

There is a real danger that the threat of change in the workplace can lead to increased levels of stress, so it is essential for your health and well-being that you are able to cope effectively – and to see the change more as a new opportunity than as a threat.

Try not to let your work concerns have too great an impact on your personal life. Talk to family and friends about the situation and allow them to help you through it.

Summary

- Change in the workplace is inevitable for a variety of often essential and unavoidable reasons.

- Change is never easy. The majority of us instinctively want things to remain the way they are. Better the devil you know!

- Common reasons for workplace change include technological, market and economic developments, merger or acquisition and corporate restructuring.

- The quicker you get yourself past the initial shock and on to the stage of accepting the change and moving on, the better.

- It is very likely that you will not be the only one to be affected by the changing circumstances, so it is important to maintain strong relationships with your peers.

- Workplace change does not have to create stress and confusion but, if you embrace the new ways of working, it can instead be seen as an opportunity.

- Remain calm and maintain a positive attitude. See change as a positive influence; find the opportunities it brings with it; embrace it.

- Undertake any necessary or available training to ensure you are able to respond effectively.

- Try not to let your work concerns have too great an impact on your personal life. Talk to family and friends about the situation and allow them to help you through it.

23

Imposing change at work

In the last chapter we discussed how to deal with having change imposed on you. In this chapter, we'll deal with imposing change from a management point of view.

Many managers, on arrival in their new job, are going to be responsible for imposing change. New managers are often required to impose changes – or should be doing so as a result of their own initiative.

It is possible for potentially negative change to be handled effectively and indeed for there to be a positive outcome. However, it is more than likely that initial reactions may be in opposition to the proposals, whilst the workforce struggles to come to terms with the potential impact of the situation. And you may well find yourself personally held to account by your new subordinates.

The effects of change

Understandably, different people will respond in different ways to workplace change, resulting in a range of mixed emotions amongst employees, one of which may be insecurity. Individuals who once felt happy and secure in their working environment may suddenly lose confidence in their employer and find themselves unsure of who they can trust – and you're unlikely to be high on their list of potential candidates for people they can trust!

The introduction of new technology to replace previously manual processes, for example, can leave people fearing redundancy, believing that they are now surplus to requirements and no longer able to carry out their job to the satisfaction of their employers – even though this may not be the case.

A lack of good communication within the organisation during a period of change can leave employees with a poor understanding of circumstances and this in turn can lead to an unwillingness to embrace or accept the new situation.

All of these emotions can have a dramatic impact on the working environment and can manifest themselves in visible alterations in behaviour:

- Motivation levels can plummet, with employees demonstrating negative attitudes.

- Productivity levels may fall, with employees being less committed and putting in fewer hours.

- Sickness and absenteeism levels may increase for both genuine reasons – and otherwise…

As a new manager, none of this is going to reflect very well on you…

The successful implementation of change

However, there are ways of successfully imposing change, ways designed to encourage a greater acceptance of change and to minimise the negative impact on the organisation.

It is your responsibility to ensure that your team is provided with effective leadership and support throughout the period of change, and to monitor their patterns of behaviour. This will enable them to ensure they are displaying positive coping strategies. There are some key guidelines which can facilitate this, including the five following points:

1 being open and honest with the workforce from the outset, explaining exactly what is going to happen and how they, as individuals, will be affected;

2 preparing a comprehensive plan to ensure the effective implementation of change in line with business objectives;

3 encouraging the team to voice their own opinions and listening carefully to their discussions;

4 getting the team actively involved in the process where appropriate and responding to positive contributions;

5 responding promptly and appropriately to any feedback you may get from the team.

Depending on the nature of the change, your organisation may also have statutory obligations of which you should be mindful. This ensures that the rights of the work-force are upheld and minimises the likelihood of future legal action.

Managing organisational change

In the past, managers have been under the misconception that change is some-thing that they simply need to impose on their employees. After all, management pays their wages, so employees should do what they are told. However, this has been shown to be a particularly negative way of implementing change. Organisational change can be extremely unsettling for all concerned and to just enforce it without first discussing the issues involved with the employees can result in a loss of trust and support.

Trying to 'sell' change is also considered to be negative. If, in effect, you are offering your employees positive rewards in the short term to obtain their support for change, it is more than likely that in the long term this will turn out to be unsustainable.

Step 1: Explain the need for change

Before you even think about implementing organisational change, your employees need to be told the reasons why change is necessary. Their view of the business may be very different from that of the managers and they may not fully understand the consequences if change is not adopted: for example, if the business stands to lose money or faces possible job cuts if changes are not taken on board immedi-ately. Also, try to ensure that the needs of the employees are aligned with those of the organisation so that everyone is working together towards the same objec-tives. As long as these needs are positive for all concerned, you should find that you can obtain the support you need from your employees for the introduction of change.

Step 2: Discuss what is involved

After you have explained why change is necessary, you should describe exactly what is going to take place. Encourage feedback and suggestions from your employees so that they feel that they are contributing to the overall direction of the organisation. This helps them to feel more motivated towards the achievement of these goals. This not only helps your employees but also allows you to see things from both perspec-tives. You may even learn something or be presented with a new idea that hadn't even occurred to you.

Step 3: Provide training and support

Some people are naturally better suited to coping with the implementation of change. However, others may be less comfortable and will benefit from the provision of training. Workshops are a really effective way of achieving understanding and encouraging group participation, and training ensures that the change is actually understood by everybody concerned – which is essential for long-term success. Use training and feedback sessions to ensure that people understand their individual role in the implementation of change and also that they are aware of how this will affect their daily responsibilities.

Step 4: Implement change

It is commonly accepted that change does not happen overnight; it can be a lengthy process that often involves a series of changes working gradually towards the achievement of the overall objective. Setting targets along the way is an effective way of making sure that the team remains motivated. Encourage managers to provide support and constructive feedback and ensure that individual and team achievements are recognised. The more positive the whole experience is, the more successful the overall process will be.

Step 5: Reinforce change

Once the change process is complete, it is important that the new systems, processes and procedures are seen to be successful. One guaranteed way of losing the support of your team is for them to feel that they have undergone a major period of upheaval for no apparent reason. Continually review the changes that have been made to make sure that they are working towards the achievement of business objectives.

Change for the sake of it

A final word of warning: You need to be very clear in your mind as to the reasoning behind the changes you're imposing. Are you sure you're not just changing things for the sake of it? Or as a result of a misguided desire to do things differently from your predecessor? Avoid change for the sake of it. Only impose changes if you have first established a firm business case for them.

Summary

- Many managers, on arrival in their new job, are going to be responsible for imposing change.

- New managers are often required to impose changes – or should be doing so as a result of their own initiative.

- It is more than likely that initial reactions may be in opposition to the proposals, whilst the workforce struggles to come to terms with the potential impact of the situation.

- A lack of good communication within the organisation during a period of change can lead to unwillingness on the part of your staff to embrace or accept the new situation.

- It is your responsibility to ensure that your team is provided with effective leadership and support throughout the period of change, and to monitor their patterns of behaviour.

- Be open and honest with the workforce from the outset, explaining exactly what is going to happen and how they, as individuals, will be affected.

- Prepare a comprehensive plan to ensure the effective implementation of change in line with business objectives.

- Encourage the team to voice their own opinions and listen carefully to their discussions.

- Get the team actively involved in the process where appropriate and respond to positive contributions.

- Explain the need for change, discuss what is involved, provide training and support, implement the change – and then reinforce that change.

- Avoid change for the sake of it. Only impose changes if you have first established a firm business case for them.

24
Feel like jumping ship?

In this chapter, we're going to discuss what you should do when your new job isn't everything you hoped it would be.

Being unhappy in your job can have a devastating effect not only on your performance at work but also on your personal life. Going to work is something that the majority of us do for many hours a week and for many years of our lives, so it is of vital importance that we strive to enjoy what we are doing.

Why are you unhappy?

If you start to feel that you are unhappy at work, you need to sit down and assess what possible reasons there may be for your dissatisfaction:

- Do you perhaps feel that your job is not very fulfilling?

- Are you not recognised for your achievements?

- Is there tension between the people you work with?

- Are you generally bored, uninspired and unchallenged?

Also, think about what is happening in your personal life; there may be something there that is making your working life less enjoyable. It is only once you have ascertained the reasons for your unhappiness that you can start to think about how best to deal with it.

How unhappy are you in your new job?

Answer yes or no to the 10 questions in this short quiz:

1 When you wake up in the morning, do you wish it was Friday already?

2 Is getting paid at the end of the week/month the best part of going to work?

3 Is coming back home again the best part of going to work?!

4 When you finish an important task do you feel relieved rather than pleased?

5 Do you feel you have little respect for your boss/the management?

6 You don't socialise with your colleagues because you spend enough time with them anyway?

7 Are you expecting your next performance appraisal to raise doubts about your commitment?

8 If you don't get a pay rise or bonus, will you immediately look for another job?

9 Are you counting the days until your next holiday?

10 Have you already found yourself looking at adverts for other jobs?

If you've answered yes to two or three questions then that's probably nothing to worry about. (I always count down the days until my next holiday!) But if you've answered yes to four or more questions then you're clearly not as happy at work as you should be – as you would like to be and as you deserve to be.

Don't act rashly

Instinctively, you may think that the best way of dealing with a job that you are not happy in is to leave it. However, this may well be a little bit hasty and there may be some changes that you can make which will improve your working life without the need for such a dramatic reaction.

For example, you may be able to take on additional responsibilities, thereby making your role more fulfilling, challenging and rewarding. You may be able to work with your current manager to establish a development plan that will help you to achieve greater satisfaction by meeting your career objectives. Alternatively, you may be able to learn new skills and undertake further training to enable you to progress further or move into a new department (more on this in the next chapter).

If your reasons for being unhappy involve conflict within your team, there are ways of addressing this that may make the situation more bearable. Seek advice from your personnel manager or from your line manager where appropriate and even try confronting the people you work with to see if the situation can be managed.

You could try making the workplace generally more fun for yourself and those around you. Organise activities or events that involve getting together with your colleagues on a more sociable level. This can be as informal as a lunchtime chat or can be a large social event. Find ways of meeting new people and of networking within your organisation; getting an insight into other functions and other roles can be refreshing. Also, try to make sure that you maintain a healthy work–life balance, a topic discussed in depth in Chapter 21, Pressure and stress.

If you feel unhappy because your working week is too long, it is important to discuss this issue with your manager to see if there is any way in which your work can be organised and prioritised more effectively. It is extremely demotivating to be spending too much time in the office and not enough time at home but often deadlines can be rearranged and workloads redistributed to enable you to enjoy the time you spend at work more.

Jumping ship

It does, of course, sometimes happen that you just cannot make any difference to your working life to enable you to get the enjoyment out of it that you need to keep you motivated. If this is the case and, if all else fails, then the time is indeed probably right for you to start looking for another job. But it is important to understand and to remember exactly what you are unhappy with so that you do not walk straight into another job in which you will be equally unhappy.

You also need to bear in mind that staying in any one job for a particularly short period of time can ring alarm bells in a recruiter's head and may take some explaining. They may conclude that you are not capable of committing yourself or of maintaining your focus. They may deem you to be fickle. It's a natural enough assumption – even if it's not justified. Be prepared to explain yourself – but without being critical of others. Criticising your current employer is considered one of the top mistakes you can make at interview and will most likely cost you the job regardless of whether or not your criticism is justified. Aim to focus on explaining the benefits you will experience in moving to your next job rather than drawing attention to the problems you had with this one.

One individual stated on his CV:

Note: Please don't misconstrue my 13 different jobs as job-hopping. I have never quit a job.

Summary

- Being unhappy in your job can have a devastating effect not only on your performance at work but also on your personal life.

- If you start to feel that you are unhappy at work, you need to sit down and assess what possible reasons there may be for your dissatisfaction.

- It is only once you have ascertained the reasons for your unhappiness that you can start to think about how best to deal with it.

- There may be some changes that you can make which will improve your working life without the need for you to get a different job.

- If all else fails and you start looking for another job, remember exactly what you are unhappy with so that you do not walk straight into another job in which you will be equally unhappy.

- You also need to bear in mind that staying in any one job for a particularly short period of time can ring alarm bells in a recruiter's head and may take some explaining.

PART SIX
ONWARDS AND UPWARDS

25
Training

If you want to progress then it's important to take a proactive approach to your own career development. Don't rely on others to manage and organise your further training; take matters into your own hands.

Training might very well be an issue you specifically covered when negotiating your original package with your new employer and you may well have a formal training allowance allocated to you.

However, whether there is or isn't a formal training structure in place with your new employer, you should go out of your way to take part in any available training, workshops or seminars that may help you to develop your skills and knowledge, and also seek to obtain support from your employer for any external training or professional qualifications.

Your employer, if they have any sense, should be keen to see you taking an active interest in the development of your career as it should mean that you are ultimately able to make a more positive contribution to the overall improvement of the organisation.

Of course, a lot of training happens 'on the job', in the course of your normal day-to-day work – and this is undoubtedly one of the most effective forms of training you can get. But you also need to give serious thought to off-the-job training, training which will not only help you in your normal day-to-day work but should help you to progress above and beyond the limits of your current role.

Identifying training possibilities

The first step towards off-the-job training is identifying and assessing the various possibilities:

- Have a word with your manager; they should be able to advise you on the opportunities available to you in this respect.

- A few minutes spent on the Internet should produce a wealth of possibilities, some more worthwhile than others.

- Flick through appropriate trade journals. These will normally carry adverts for relevant training opportunities.

- Bear in mind that training will generally require quite a significant commitment of time and effort (and maybe even money) on your part.

- Thoroughly and carefully examine the various options before reaching a decision.

- Reaching out to your network for advice could be very much worth your while.

Professional qualifications

Besides less formal training such as participation in workshops, you should also be looking to see if you can achieve more highly recognised qualifications. So-called 'professional qualifications' are increasingly popular in the workplace, both as an alternative to formal academic qualifications and in addition to them. Professional qualifications are recognised as not only providing an individual with industry-specific skills but also as being a demonstration of the individual's commitment to continuous learning and development. Skills acquired through many professional qualifications can also be transferred to other functional areas and are a valuable tool to facilitate career development. Some organisations have even been known to offer bonuses or incentives to employees willing to undertake relevant professional qualifications.

Certain industries have now made professional qualifications an essential requirement and many employers will provide full support, enabling them to be completed alongside normal work responsibilities. Studying for professional qualifications can be undertaken on a full- or part-time basis and can even be completed via distance learning. Employers often allow time off for professional studies and may also assist with the payment of necessary fees. It is worth remembering, however, that if an employer is supporting you during your studies, this will probably mean that you will be tied into your employment with them for the duration of your studies.

As well as improving your chances of securing internal promotions, professional qualifications can add considerable value to your CV when you are actively seeking employment. They tend to indicate that a candidate has specific skills and experiences, rather than just academic and theoretical knowledge. Qualifications such as NVQs, for example, are applicable to a wide variety of industries and involve workplace assessments aimed at verifying your actual on-the-job competence. Other increasingly popular professional qualifications include the European Computer Driving Licence (ECDL) and the RSA Computer Literacy and Information Technology (CLAIT) qualification. Many roles involving computer-based administration may well require a candidate to have completed one of these qualifications, or similar, because although many people claim to be proficient in the use of computers, these qualifications are considered by employers to actually prove it.

Professional memberships

Many industry sectors now offer the opportunity to become a member of a professional organisation. There are a number of levels achievable for membership status and the highest status can only be achieved once a candidate has demonstrated that they have completed appropriate training and spent a significant period of their working life within the industry sector. Training and employment history both need to be correctly logged and verified before accreditation can be awarded and, although this process obviously takes some considerable time, fast-track options are becoming available in some industries.

Becoming a member of a professional organisation provides external recognition and may also offer reassurance to customers that they are dealing with someone whose behaviour and conduct are regulated. Once professional status has been awarded, you are also expected to maintain and develop your skills and knowledge by undertaking any further training that is available. There are usually specific guidelines which must be adhered to and, in some cases of extreme non-compliance, professional status can be withdrawn.

Summary

- If you want to progress then it's important to take a proactive approach to your own career development.

- You should go out of your way to take part in any available training, workshops or seminars that may help you to develop your skills and knowledge.

- You should also seek to obtain support from your employer for any external training or professional qualifications.

- Besides less formal training such as participation in workshops, you should also be looking to see if you can achieve more highly recognised qualifications.

- So-called 'professional qualifications' are increasingly popular in the workplace, both as an alternative to formal academic qualifications and in addition to them.

- Many industry sectors now offer the opportunity to become a member of a professional organisation.

- Becoming a member of a professional organisation provides external recognition and may also offer reassurance to customers that they are dealing with someone whose behaviour and conduct are regulated.

26
Performance appraisals

A time will come when you're beyond the first few days, weeks and months of your new job, you've settled in and found your place – and it's time to look to the future.

Not all organisations operate a formal system of performance appraisals but most organisations will appraise your performance in one way or another at certain intervals. There are many different types of performance appraisal, ranging from a quick chat with the boss over a cup of tea to a more rigid – and documented – appraisal, typical of larger organisations. This chapter will inevitably focus on the latter – because it's clearly the latter which is the greater challenge!

The aim of performance appraisals

The thought of a forthcoming performance appraisal can be enough to send shivers down the spine of even the most hardened professional. It's a lot like a job interview – and it's natural to be a little apprehensive. Appraisals can be seen as an opportunity for your manager to voice their gripes and dissatisfaction and to generally criticise. However, the true and proper aim of a performance appraisal is to motivate and develop an employee and, if approached correctly by you and your manager, there is no reason why the whole experience cannot be both rewarding and positive. A good manager should try to make your appraisal reasonably informal and non-confrontational.

Preparation

As always, preparation is key. You should be given plenty of time to prepare for the appraisal and you should use this time constructively rather than just anxiously waiting for the day to come.

Formal performance appraisals are generally carried out on an annual basis but you must, of course, remember that your performance and achievements throughout the entire year will be under assessment. Evidence of your overall contribution to the organisation will be reviewed, as will your level of success in the achievement of your targets and objectives. To help yourself prepare for your appraisal, it is helpful for you to keep comprehensive records of exactly what you have achieved through-out the year and anything relating to your individual performance.

Another useful preparation tip is to read through your original job description, highlighting how you have fulfilled your duties and responsibilities and what you have achieved which you feel exceeds the demands of your core role. Pay particular attention to any challenges that you were faced with during the course of the year, detailing exactly how you were able to overcome them. Don't be shy or overly modest. It's not the time for that. If you think that you succeeded particularly well in a certain field then say so and be comfortable with discussing it.

In the last chapter we discussed the importance of ongoing training. Make sure that you keep complete records of all the development opportunities you have seized and bring these with you to the performance appraisal.

Setting benchmarks

It is in your mutual interest that the targets you agree with your manager are realis-tic, otherwise you can become demotivated, resulting in an overall decline in your performance. The specific targets and objectives that are set for you will be used to form the basis of your overall action plan – and will be used as a benchmark in your next appraisal. This action plan should also take into account your long-term career aspirations, to enable you to effectively develop your career in the appropri-ate direction. For example, it may well highlight future training requirements – and now is the ideal time to get that subject on the table whilst you've got your manager's full and undivided attention. Your finalised action plan is a very important docu-ment and you should refer back to it on a regular basis in order to monitor your performance and ongoing development. It'll also come in very handy when you're preparing for your next appraisal. It will help you to assess whether or not (and to what degree) you have achieved the specific targets and objectives set for you by your manager.

Dealing with negative issues

A performance appraisal should really be a positive activity and is not the appropriate time for your manager to discuss serious grievances or disciplinary matters. However, you may well face some criticism and, whilst this may not be pleasant, as long as it is well founded and constructive you should try to handle this as positively and professionally as you can. Don't be seen to be on the defensive but try instead to cooperate with your manager and work through the issues with them, paying close attention to any advice they may give you. Be seen to take on board both their positive and their negative comments.

You should bear in mind that it's also a useful opportunity to raise any aspects of your role in which you might have had difficulties so that you can discuss with your manager how matters can be improved for the year ahead. It's easy to think that it's a one-way conversation when it's most definitely not – all meetings should be very much two-way conversations. By discussing any weaknesses you may have, your manager can help you to find appropriate solutions for overcoming them.

A win–win situation

Performance appraisals are not just for your manager's benefit. For you, they should be a valuable tool to fine-tune your ongoing career development – and can be used to support requests for pay rises and promotion (which we'll be discussing in further detail in the next couple of chapters).

If handled effectively by both you and your manager, performance appraisals should help to reinforce a positive relationship between you, improving the way you communicate and being of mutual benefit.

Possible questions

Your manager could ask you a very wide array of different questions. You may even wish to refer to a good book on interview technique (please see Further reading and resources at the end of this book) to give you ideas as to some of the questions you might be asked and how best to handle them. Here are a dozen common possibilities which you must definitely consider in advance of your appraisal:

- What has been the best part of your job in the past year – and why?

- What has been your biggest disappointment in the past year – and why?

- How do you feel you have delivered and added value to your role in the past year?

- What new skills and abilities do you feel you have developed in the past year?

- What procedures, policies, systems, etc could do with improvement?

- What further training options would you like to see us offering?

- What one single thing would you like to change about your current role?

- How best do you personally like to be recognised and rewarded for performance?

- Do you feel you're being managed too closely or not closely enough?

- Where would you like to see yourself being a year from now?

- What is it that convinces you to stay working with us and not look elsewhere?

- What would convince you to take another job elsewhere?

Just as in a job interview, you'll also want to have prepared some questions of your own. The questions you choose to ask will depend to a degree on the questions you actually get asked. But here are a dozen useful ideas for you:

- What do you think has been my greatest strength in the past year?

- What do you think has been my greatest weakness in the past year?

- What one area do you think I should concentrate on to improve my performance?

- What are your/the organisation's key goals for the year ahead?

- What can I do to be better able to help you/the organisation achieve those goals?

- What do you see as my top priorities for the next six months?

- What changes could I make that would make me/your job easier to manage?

- What do you think I should be doing that I'm not doing already?

- What are my possibilities for promotion within the organisation?

- From what kind of training or professional development do you think I could benefit?

- How do you anticipate my role evolving over the next two to three years?

- How do you see the organisation evolving over the next five years?

It would be a mistake not to ask any questions; you'll just come across as passive and uninterested. However, at the same time, avoid asking too many questions – and certainly avoid asking questions just for the sake of it. Choose your questions wisely.

Finally, remember to thank your manager for their time before you leave. Good manners go a long way!

Summary

- Not all organisations operate a formal system of performance appraisals but most organisations will appraise your performance in one way or another at certain intervals.

- The true and proper aim of a performance appraisal is to motivate and develop an employee and there is no reason why the whole experience cannot be both rewarding and positive.

- You should be given plenty of time to prepare for the appraisal and you should use this time constructively rather than just anxiously waiting for the day to come.

- It is helpful for you to keep comprehensive records of exactly what you have achieved throughout the year and anything relating to your individual performance.

- Read through your original job description, highlighting how you have fulfilled your duties and responsibilities and what you have achieved.

- It is in your mutual interest that the targets you agree with your manager are realistic, otherwise you can become demotivated, resulting in an overall decline in your performance.

- It's easy to think that it's a one-way conversation when it's most definitely not – all meetings should be very much two-way conversations.

- By discussing any weaknesses you may have, your manager can help you to find appropriate solutions for overcoming them.

27
Time for a pay rise?

If you're progressing well in your new job, you're most likely going to want to be rewarded for it, either with a pay rise or possibly by achieving a promotion.

In this chapter we're going to deal with how to successfully handle a request for a pay rise. We'll come to handling a request for a promotion in the next chapter.

Requesting a pay rise

If you feel you have advanced in your role to the point where you should be paid more, then your first step should always be to address the issue with your manager. There is every chance that a mutually agreeable solution can be reached.

This is no shame in asking for a pay rise. Whilst your employer might not be delighted by the prospect, they should respect that you are entirely within your rights to make such a request. If you feel you're no longer being paid what you're worth then you're perfectly entitled to speak up and say so. Ultimately, you could be doing your employer a favour. Rather than looking elsewhere for work and then just handing in your resignation, you are giving your employer a chance to review your remuneration and make an appropriate effort to retain your services.

I won't claim that they'll greet your request with open arms, though!

Timing

Timing can be a very important factor when asking for a pay rise. It can have a significant impact on your chances of success.

Clearly it would be a mistake to demand a pay rise too soon after starting a new job (or too soon after your last pay rise). You need to allow yourself time to make sufficient impact to warrant a pay rise. Conversely, you shouldn't leave it too long either. You deserve to be paid what you're worth – and not to have your remuneration eroded by inflation.

Many organisations automatically review salaries on an annual basis – and quite possibly at the same time as they undertake your performance appraisal. However, if 12 months pass and there's no sign that a pay rise is forthcoming then it's very possibly time for you to seize the initiative.

You still need to choose your moment carefully, though. Try to pick a time when your contribution to the organisation is going to be seen in the best possible light. If you're halfway through a major project then wait until its successful completion. If you're working on a tender for a big contract then wait until you've won the contract. If you've recently taken on new duties or responsibilities then wait until you've demonstrated that you have risen to the challenge.

You also need to bear in mind other factors which could impact on the timing of your request. If your organisation is currently experiencing financial difficulties then your request may well be frowned upon. If your boss is under an unusual amount of stress – or is experiencing personal problems of some sort – then, again, you would be well advised to postpone your request until things have settled back down.

Tact and diplomacy

It's obvious enough that putting in a request for a pay rise can be a delicate matter.

Whilst receiving a letter of resignation is undoubtedly worse for an employer, receiving a request for a pay rise is not exactly good news either. A lot therefore depends on how precisely you phrase your request.

I'm not just talking about your chances of successfully negotiating the pay rise, I'm also – and perhaps more importantly – talking about the relationship you have with your current employer.

If you get it right then it's not going to guarantee you a pay rise but it will at least minimise the chances of your damaging your relationship with your employer in any way.

TOP TIP

You're going to need to approach the issue of a pay rise tactfully and handle any subsequent negotiations diplomatically if you don't want to sour your relationship with your employer.

Whilst it's fine to have confidence in yourself – and in your right to make such a request – you should definitely avoid coming across as demanding. If you're asking for more money then the onus is clearly on you to make a persuasive case – but do act respectfully at all times.

Proving your value

Simply asking for more money for doing the same job is generally unlikely to go down well with an employer. Instead, you need to try to demonstrate to the employer the contribution you make to their organisation over and above their core expectations. You need to demonstrate what you've achieved. You need to demonstrate what you're really worth:

- What progress have you made since you started your current role?

- What value do you add to the organisation which warrants a higher level of remuneration?

- What examples can you cite to back up your claims?

The answers to these questions will be different for everyone. You need to think through your own answers – clearly and concisely – because they will be fundamental to the 'pitch' you make to your employer. Only by proving your value can you hope to prove your case for a rise.

You might think it should be blatantly obvious to your boss what you've achieved – but don't count on it! You still need to spell out your case.

What to ask for

What exactly do you want to ask for? You could, of course, state the precise number of pound notes you're expecting. However, I wouldn't recommend this strategy.

The best approach is to request a face-to-face meeting. This will give both you and your employer the opportunity to enter into a two-way dialogue, lay all your cards on the table and, with a bit of luck, reach a solution you are both happy with.

I would suggest you take a few minutes to read through Chapter 1, Handling the offer, so as to acquaint yourself with the basics of such negotiations. Whilst not all of the advice is relevant to this situation, a lot of the basic principles remain the same.

Avoiding threats

The thought of backing up your request with a threat might not even have crossed your mind. However, many employees – rather ill-advisedly – believe it to be a good negotiating tactic to threaten that they might be 'forced' to look for another job if their request isn't accepted. Such threats might be made very directly or they might just be subtly implied. But my advice is to make sure that you don't make any threat of any sort.

Nobody likes to be threatened and an employer might well see this as blackmail – something they definitely won't respond to favourably. Yes, it's conceivable they may give in to this in the short term but, in the long term, your relationship with them will be permanently scarred.

You should focus very much on what you currently do for your employer – not what you will do if they fail to give you what you want.

An example of a letter requesting a pay rise is provided in Figure 27.1.

FIGURE 27.1 Letter requesting a pay rise

Joe Bloggs
1 Anyold Road
ANYWHERE
AN1 1CV
telephone: 01632 960 603 / 07700 900 790
e-mail: joebloggs@example.com

Mr Malcolm Smith
IT Director
The CV Centre Limited
1 Liverpool Street
LONDON
EC2M 7QD

1 March 2012

Dear Malcolm

Remuneration review request

I am writing to request the opportunity for a review of my current remuneration.

It has now been just over a year since I took up my role as the company's Web Developer. In that time, I feel that I have made a very significant contribution to the company which warrants a reconsideration of the salary package I currently receive.

The systems I have put in place to collect potential sales leads online make a major contribution to the results of the sales team – these days more and more of our new business comes via the website. And, by identifying ways to attract potential new employees online, I have contributed to a reduction in the amount we spend on recruitment consultants – again resulting in a direct impact on the company's bottom line.

Most recently, I have completed an extensive site redesign which has seen our online sales conversion rate rise by approximately 17 per cent. Since our marketing costs in this respect remain constant, the overall effect on profits is significant.

In view of the above, I would be grateful if we could timetable a meeting to discuss my role and my remuneration in greater detail.

I look forward to hearing from you and thank you for your time.

Kind regards

Joe Bloggs

Summary

- Whilst your employer might not be delighted by your asking for a pay rise, they should respect that you are entirely within your rights to make such a request.

- Try to pick a time when your contribution to the organisation is going to be seen in the best possible light.

- If you get it right then it's not going to guarantee you a pay rise but it will at least minimise the chances of your damaging your relationship with your employer in any way.

- You're going to need to approach the matter tactfully and handle any subsequent negotiations diplomatically if you don't want to sour this relationship.

- You need to try to demonstrate to the employer the contribution you make to their organisation over and above their core expectations.

- Only by proving your value can you hope to prove your case for a rise.

- Avoid making any threat of any sort – for example, suggesting that you might be 'forced' to look for another job if your request isn't accepted.

- Focus on what you currently do for your employer – not what you will do if they fail to give you what you want.

28
Getting promoted

In many cases, the best way to progress to a more challenging role – a position with greater responsibility and autonomy – is to look for a new job. This is one of the top reasons why people want to change jobs.

However, this doesn't necessarily mean that your new job needs to be with a different organisation.

If you're happy working for your current employer but are simply no longer satisfied with the role you play in the organisation, then the ideal situation could be to be awarded a promotion – rather than have to go through all the upheaval of moving to a different organisation.

Opportunities for promotion

You may already have identified a suitable vacancy:

- Perhaps one has been advertised internally.

- Possibly someone in a more senior position has decided to leave or retire.

- Maybe a new branch, department or division is opening up.

- Your company could be tendering for a major new contract.

In such cases, your approach should not be too dissimilar to applying for any new job. Don't make the mistake of thinking that just because you are already known to the organisation, you don't need to put together a comprehensive and compelling application.

The speculative approach

In many cases, however, you might not perceive a specific opportunity and may just be enquiring on a purely speculative basis. As such, there is of course no guarantee that a suitable position will be available with your current employer. A lot can depend on the size of the organisation – but it's definitely always worth a shot.

TOP TIP

Even if there isn't a position immediately available, you will be demonstrating your desire to progress and when a more senior position does become available your name could be first on the list. And in the meantime there's always the possibility that your employer might try to 'pacify' you with a pay rise!

One possibility is that your request will prompt your employer to seek ways in which they can change or add to your role so that you feel more fulfilled – again with an accompanying pay rise if appropriate.

From an employer's point of view, someone who wants a promotion is someone who is at risk of leaving unless they are able to find ways to accommodate the person's needs. One way or the other, if you're a valued employee, your employer is likely to make some effort to improve your situation.

Ten top tips to win a promotion

Achieving promotion is about consistent strong performance over time but, in the run up to your seeking promotion, you'll need to make even more effort than usual. Here are my top 10 tips for winning yourself a promotion:

1 Behave like the new broom you once were. Make sure you don't arrive for work late. Dress to impress. Be on your very best behaviour! Image is everything.

2 Give 110 per cent. Strive for excellence. You may be able to get away with less in the normal day-to-day run of things but not when you're after a promotion.

3 Ensure your work can't be faulted. Work carefully and meticulously. Don't 'drop the ball', miss deadlines, etc. Prove you're someone who gets the job done.

4 Seize every opportunity to learn something new and to develop and enhance your skills and knowledge base.

5 If at all possible, start taking on new and additional responsibilities in your existing role. Show initiative and commitment. Volunteer for new assignments.

6 If you're applying to step up to a management or team leadership role then start consciously acting the part now – without stepping on anyone's toes!

7 Now might well be the time to consider putting in some more time. Seriously consider any overtime opportunities that might arise.

8 Update your CV (please see the next chapter for further details); at the very least it'll help to get you in the right frame of mind to successfully tackle the job promotion interview.

9 Identify and resolve any blockers which might be holding you back. Are there any little holes in your skill set or any aspects of your performance which might be a problem?

10 As a general rule, make it easy for the organisation to promote you. Make it into a logical, sensible and beneficial decision for them. Make it the right decision.

Why do you deserve a promotion?

So, why exactly do you deserve a promotion? If it was just going to be handed to you on a plate then your employer would already have done it. No, you're going to need to justify your request – and you're going to need to do so persuasively. It's not too dissimilar to applying for a pay rise (please see the previous chapter for more on requesting a pay rise).

The main thrust of your pitch should be to communicate to your employer how you have developed in ways which now warrant your promotion to a more senior position. The message you're sending is that you've mastered the requirements of your current role and, as a consequence, it is now no longer a sufficient challenge for you.

Don't fall into the trap of underselling yourself. Approach your application as forcefully as you would if you were applying for a job with a different organisation. There's nothing wrong with blowing your own trumpet – because you can't rely on anyone else to do so!

Start with an overview of your time with the organisation and outline succinctly the progress you have made in that time. You should also make mention of any formal training you have undertaken since you were first appointed to the role.

Conclude by specifying the kind of role to which you would now hope to be appointed.

An example of a letter requesting promotion is provided in Figure 28.1.

FIGURE 28.1   Letter requesting a promotion

Joe Bloggs
1 Anyold Road
ANYWHERE
AN1 1CV
telephone: 01632 960 603 / 07700 900 790
e-mail: joebloggs@example.com

Mr Paul Geary
Customer Services Director
The CV Centre Limited
1 Liverpool Street
LONDON
EC2M 7QD

1 March 2012

Dear Mr Geary

Promotion request

I am writing to enquire whether there is any opportunity for my promotion to a more senior role.

Over the course of my past three years with the company, I believe I have developed my skills and experience in numerous different ways. I have matured as an individual and my experience of working with others – both colleagues and customers – has contributed a lot to my interpersonal skills. I am also better able to see the bigger picture and how the function of my department relates to the overall goals of the organisation.

Recently I have undertaken an evening course in business administration which has further helped to shape the way I work and has given a formal structure to many of the skills I have developed on a practical basis.

As a result of the above, I am now much more productive in my role – and much better equipped to help my colleagues to handle unusual or difficult situations. I therefore feel the time is right for me to step up to a management-level position and I would be pleased to discuss any opportunities which may be available.

I look forward to hearing from you and thank you for your time.

Yours sincerely

Joe Bloggs

The job promotion interview

If your employer is able to offer you the possibility of a promotion then you can expect to be interviewed for the role in question.

A job promotion interview has many similarities with any other job interview. However, it also has a number of differences.

You should be able to prepare particularly well for potential questions because your knowledge of the job and the organisation should be far greater than someone coming in from outside the organisation. And you should bear in mind that you may well be up against candidates coming from outside the organisation. Don't put in any less effort just because you're an 'inside' candidate.

You will have access to people who can help you to prepare for the interview – for example, your future peers and colleagues. Maybe the promotion is becoming available as a result of someone else leaving the role? Seize the opportunity to sit down and have a good talk with them about it; identify opportunities, challenges and problems which you can later discuss at interview. If you can demonstrate to your interviewer that you can really hit the ground running then that will give you an inevitable advantage over outside candidates.

The biggest difference is, of course, quite simply the fact that you will more than likely know your interviewer – and they are likely to think they know you! However, this doesn't mean you should put in any less effort than you would if you were applying for a new job in a different organisation. The little details like dressing correctly, controlling your body language, making a powerful first impression, being enthusiastic, etc all apply equally. You need to bridge the gap between their current perception of you and the perception they need to have of you if they are to appoint you to a higher position.

You can expect to face a variety of questions – just as in any interview – and I'd suggest you refer to a good book on interview technique for further help. Please see Further reading and resources at the end of this book.

Money, money, money

There is, initially, no need to bring up the subject of money when requesting a promotion. Your focus should be on your moving to a role which is more rewarding in and of itself, rather than just more rewarding in financial terms.

Most employers will be fully aware that, if they are to promote you, you will naturally be expecting an accompanying pay rise. However, this can be discussed later – possibly even after you have taken up your new role and had a chance to prove yourself.

Summary

- If you're no longer satisfied with the role you play in an organisation, then the ideal situation could be to be awarded a promotion.

- You may already have identified a suitable vacancy and, in such cases, your approach should not be too dissimilar to applying for any new job.

- Even if you haven't identified a specific vacancy, it's always worth a shot to write on a speculative basis.

- Whilst there may not be a position immediately available, you will nevertheless be demonstrating your desire to progress.

- Your request may also prompt your employer to seek ways in which they can change or add to your role so that you feel more fulfilled.

- You're going to need to justify your request by communicating to your employer how you have developed in ways which now warrant your promotion.

- Succinctly outline the progress you have made and be sure to make mention of any formal training you have undertaken since you were first appointed.

- Conclude by specifying the kind of role to which you would now hope to be appointed.

29
Moving on

Sooner or later, a time will come when you wish to move on. Whatever your reasons, your first step will be to create an interview-winning CV – and that will be the subject of this chapter.

'Curriculum vitae' is a Latin term and translates as 'the course of one's life'. The simplest dictionary definition says that a curriculum vitae is 'a summary of your academic and work history'. Well, that's basically true, but I see a curriculum vitae (commonly abbreviated, of course, to 'CV') as more of a personal sales brochure, one which should be very carefully written and presented to ensure you have the best possible chance of getting the job you want – to really showcase your talent.

It is not an autobiography. Simply writing down a list of everything you have done and everything you know will not guarantee you an interview – in fact, it will just bore the socks off the recruiter and undoubtedly count against you.

You should never lose sight of the fact that the primary aim of your CV is purely and simply to win you an interview.

Laying the foundations: getting the basics right

It is vitally important to see matters from the recruiter's or prospective employer's perspective.

They're often faced with a pile of many hundreds of CVs to review – for just one vacancy. Almost a third of recruiters admit to only reading a CV for a minute before deciding whether to interview the candidate. In fact, many admit to spending even less time – 20 to 30 seconds is quite common.

They simply do not have the time to read them all in any depth. They're much more interested in getting out of the office and getting down the pub! In their initial sift, they will very likely be looking for reasons to discard your application, not for reasons to retain it. So how do you make your CV stand out? How do you maximise your chances of being amongst the 10 or so candidates they decide to invite for interview?

You need to determine exactly what to put in, exactly what to leave out, and what kind of a 'spin' to put on your CV, to ensure that yours will stand right out from your competition. Getting it right is the difference between getting your foot in the door for an interview, or ending up in the 'No, thank you' pile – also known as the bin!

You need to help the recruiter as much as possible since they see sifting through CVs as a chore and want it to be over as quickly as possible (remember, there's that pint waiting for them down the road!). They do not know you and they don't know what you're capable of – this is where you have to sell yourself.

The 15 most common CV writing mistakes – and how to avoid them!

The CV Centre has conducted a comprehensive analysis of over 2,500 CVs to derive a Top 15 of the common mistakes people make:

1. Inclusion of photographs

People often include photos of themselves on their CV. Don't! Unless you are applying to be a model or wish to work as an actor/actress then including a photo with/on your CV is definitely not recommended – at least not within the UK. (They're much more common elsewhere in the world.)

2. Inappropriate heading

Your CV should be headed with your name – and just your name – boldly and clearly – before any other details – contact details, etc. It should not be headed 'Curriculum vitae' or 'CV' or anything else. Just your name (and only your first name and last name).

3. Missing or inappropriate e-mail addresses

Whilst not having an e-mail address at all on your CV is clearly a problem, it's not something I see very often. Far more common is the use of fun or jokey e-mail addresses. Whilst these may be fine for corresponding with friends and family, employers will probably regard more 'serious' e-mail addresses as simply more professional.

4. Superfluous personal details at the top of the CV

My clients often feel that it is compulsory to include details such as their marital status, nationality, number (and ages) of children/dependants, etc. Whilst, yes, it certainly used to be the norm to include this sort of information on a CV, it is now increasingly rare, given modern anti-discrimination legislation, to find these sorts of details on a CV. They simply aren't relevant.

5. Lack of clear section headings/separation of sections

It is vitally important for your CV to be easy for the reader to scan quickly and, to this end, clear section headings and separation of sections is essential. I often recommend the use of lines or other graphic devices in this respect, although there are other ways of achieving a clearer separation.

6. Writing in the first person

The words 'I' and 'me' are often used repeatedly in home-made CVs. CVs should be written exclusively in the third person. Making a CV too personal by using 'I' and 'me' tends to look unprofessional. It can convey an impression of arrogance and egocentrism: 'I this...', 'I that...', 'I the other...', 'me, me, me!' But most of all it's just too informal. It might seem unnatural to write a document about yourself and yet never use either 'I' or 'me' but recruitment experts conclusively agree that this is the best way to do it.

7. Lack of proper professional profile and/or objective

It is very important to include a sufficiently detailed and very carefully phrased professional profile and, if space permits, objective at the beginning of the CV. The reader needs to know instantly what you're about and what sort of position you are looking for. This is also a key area to consider tailoring for different applications. It's one of the first (and sometimes only) sections the reader will see and consequently gives you a vital opportunity to make a powerful first impression on them.

8. Inappropriate section order

It's extremely important to choose an appropriate order for the various sections of your CV. For example, the decision whether to put your education and qualifications before or after your career history is critical. It all depends on which is your greater selling point. You should make sure that all your most important information is conveyed on the first page or, for a one-page CV, in the top half of the page.

9. No bullet pointing

In today's fast-paced world, recruiters no longer have the time to read large, solid blocks of prose. They need to extract the information they need – and they need to do it fast. Long paragraphs of prose are tiresome for a recruiter to read right through and, as a result, many simply won't bother. And this is where bullet pointing comes in, although, unfortunately, so many people fail to use it to their advantage within their CV.

10. Reverse chronological order not used

It is a standard convention on CVs to use reverse chronological order, ie to present your most recent information first, followed by older – and consequently less relevant – information. And I would strongly suggest you make sure your CV conforms to this.

11. Excessive details of interests

You should aim to keep your interests section brief. As with every other aspect of your CV, do include what you feel will count in your favour – but be selective about it. Many people write far too much in this section.

12. Date of birth included

I often get asked whether or not you should include your date of birth (or age) on a CV. The old answer to this used to be that you should include it, because recruiters expect to see it and so if you don't include it then it'll just draw attention to the fact. However, this advice has now changed – since the introduction of the Employment Equality (Age) Regulations 2006.

13. Referees included

Details of referees generally shouldn't be included on your CV. They're a waste of valuable space! They clutter it up and, more importantly, you will find that your referees get pestered unnecessarily by time wasters. By the time they have handled their umpteenth enquiry of the day, they are a lot less likely to say nice things about you!

14. Spelling, grammar and typos

Our research has shown that 60 per cent of the CVs we receive contain linguistic errors. It is impossible to stress enough how important this issue is. Spelling and grammatical errors are amongst the most irritating errors a recruiter sees – and also amongst the most easily avoided. The answer is to check, check and check again.

15. Length

This is one of the most common problems I see when people prepare their own CVs – they're quite simply too long. This is not an autobiography you're writing. It's a curriculum vitae. It's a lot shorter!

My five top tips to make your CV stand out

Make an effort to accommodate these five points when writing your CV and you'll immediately be well above average:

1 *Maximise readability*. It is essential for your CV to be easy for the reader to scan quickly and effectively. You need to separate different sections and insert clear section headings. Avoid long paragraphs; use bullet pointing to break up text into more manageable 'bite-size' chunks. It should be eye-catching and uncluttered. Check vigilantly for spelling and grammatical errors.

2 *Include a professional profile and objective*. These sections should summarise and emphasise your key attributes and your intended future career path. Your words must flow seamlessly – avoiding cliché and superfluous hyperbole.

3 *Include achievements where possible*. If you can include an achievements section then it can make an instant and dramatic difference to the power of your CV, enabling you to distinguish yourself from other candidates.

4 *Keep your CV concise and to the point*. Your CV should be informative – but also concise. In general, two A4 pages is a maximum. Too many CVs are quite simply too long. Only include information which will actually help to sell you. Recruiters don't want to waste time reading details irrelevant to your ability to fulfil the job role.

5 *Target/tailor your CV*. If possible, tailor your CV according to the specific vacancy for which you are applying. A carefully targeted CV can easily mean the difference between success and failure.

CV templates

Writing a professional CV is obviously easier said than done, so here are a few example CVs which should help to illustrate all the points I make above – and which should also help you to generate lots of useful ideas for your own CV.

Whilst these examples are based on real-life CVs which have helped my clients to win interviews, I have blended together several CVs so as to better demonstrate key principles – and most of the fine details have been changed to preserve my clients' anonymity. These CVs therefore don't represent real people and their real careers but they do represent the presentation, content, structure and style you should be aiming for when writing your own CV.

These examples obviously include lots of formatting which it might be hard for you to copy from this book – or at the very least rather time-consuming to do so. I have therefore provided a special link for you to go online and download a full set of CV and cover letter templates. There's no charge for this. All readers of *Ultimate New Job* are entitled to this entirely for free.

Simply visit the following page to quickly and easily download your free templates: **www.ineedacv.co.uk/templates**.

FIGURE 29.1

Alexandra Cooper

1 Any Road, Anytown AN1 1CV
Telephone: 07700 900 389
E-mail: alexandracooper@example.com

Professional profile

A highly qualified MBA student with a unique combination of skills and capabilities acquired during studies and work experience. Able to demonstrate strong customer focus combined with a proven commitment to the achievement of targets and business objectives. Works effectively on own initiative with the organisation and time management required to complete assignments on time and to the required quality standard. Enjoys being part of a successful and productive team and thrives in highly pressurised and challenging working environments.

Objective

Currently looking to secure a marketing internship within a forward-thinking organisation, one that will make best use of existing skills and experience while enabling further personal and professional development.

Education and qualifications

MBA: Master's in Business Administration (graduate October 2009)
            MASTA London School of Business (accredited by University of Scotland)

MSc: Biotechnology (2007)
            Paramedical College, Whalgar University, Calcutta, India

---

BSc:	Biotechnology, Chemistry and Zoology (2005)
	Kanpur University, Kanpur, India
Intermediate:	Physics, Chemistry, Biology, English and Computer Science (2002)
High School:	Mathematics, Science, Social Science, English and Hindi (2000)

Further skills

| **IT Proficiency:** | Word, Excel, C++, Internet and e-mail |
| **Languages:** | Fluent English and Hindi; currently learning French |

Work experience

2007–2009   Customer Care Officer, Pensions R Us Ltd

- Providing information and advice to employees of several major US hotel chains regarding their pensions plans
- Advising on the availability of suitable pension plans and assisting with the transfer of plans from one fund to another

Interests and activities

Currently include: Photography, drawing, reading (autobiographies and science journals), swimming, football and badminton

References are available on request

FIGURE 29.2

Sᴀʀᴀʜ Hᴇᴘᴡᴏʀᴛʜ

1 Any Road, Anytown AN1 1CV

Telephone: 01632 960 551

Mobile: 07700 900 481

Fax: 01632 960 656

E-mail: sarahhepworth@example.com

PROFESSIONAL PROFILE

A resourceful, hard-working and dedicated individual with outstanding administrative and organisational skills and the proven ability to develop and implement effective new systems and procedures. Possesses excellent IT skills with advanced knowledge of MS Office, is quick to grasp new ideas and concepts and always keen to develop new skills and expertise. Able to work well both independently and as part of a productive team, demonstrating the motivation and multi-tasking abilities required to meet demanding deadlines while maintaining the highest of standards. Articulate and proactive, combines a professional and confident approach with excellent interpersonal skills and can communicate concisely at all levels.

CAREER SUMMARY

2006–date   Business Improvement Project Coordinator, Luton Ltd, London

- Working as PA to the Programme Director with responsibility for developing, implementing and monitoring efficient office activities in addition to managing all correspondence
- Undertaking diary and event management and making travel arrangements as well as organising meetings with associated catering and accommodation
- Providing effective secretarial support and managing holiday requests and absence due to sickness for the project team and overseeing the office facilities
- Responsible as Project Coordinator for delivering a number of systems enhancements within the business improvement programme
- Consulting with staff at all levels to identify policy and best practice requirements as well as managing the Policy & Best Practice intranet site
- Making key contributions to the management of the communication plan while monitoring and updating programme plans on a wider basis
- Liaising with individual project teams to ensure the delivery of objectives while tracking the overall project progress and deliverables
- Preparing comprehensive consolidated project status and performance reports for the OpEx team

CAREER SUMMARY cont.

2005–2006   PA/Office Manager, Leonardo plc, Godalming

- Undertaking PA duties including diary management for the IT Director in addition to managing team expenses, diaries and schedules and the IT budget
- Coordinating travel and accommodation arrangements as well as managing meeting schedules and organising lunches and refreshments
- Creating a range of documentation including presentations, correspondence, memos and reports as well as taking minutes when required, and providing secretarial support for the team and management
- Carrying out IT procurement activities, monitoring third-party suppliers to ensure consistently good value as well as maintaining the IT standard catalogue
- Overseeing the smooth operation of the procurement process, managing work queues and evaluating performance tracking activities
- Compiling reports highlighting costs of products and services as well as preparing data for forecasting and budgeting
- Undertaking office management activities with responsibility for stationery, equipment and company mobile phones as well as organising company and rental vehicles
- Keeping accurate records of holiday and absence in addition to establishing data tracking systems and developing efficient office procedures

2003–2005   Sales and Training Coordinator, Simon Says Leisure, Woking

- Working in a sales analyst role, preparing daily and monthly spreadsheets on behalf of the sales team and creating sales and performance graphs, sales and marketing presentations
- Maintaining the sales database as well as producing business reports on sales and income from membership joining fees and reconciling monthly commissions and quarterly bonuses
- Coordinating training activities, managing an online training diary and organising training events as well as preparing training packs and issuing joining instructions
- Delivering administrative support in sales and marketing as well as collating the training report on a monthly basis and organising accommodation, travel and refreshments as required

2000–2003   Business Support Executive, Graphic Office Supplies, Guildford

- Developing and delivering the online ordering system and training internal staff in its use in addition to providing administration of online accounts and the back-office system
- Demonstrating the online system to customers before closing sales, following up with system training as required
- Compiling online tutorials and training packs as well as providing full helpdesk support for the system

CAREER SUMMARY cont.

1998–2000   **PA/Marketing Coordinator, Anarchy Ltd, Winchester**

- Providing comprehensive PA support for the Sales and Marketing Director in addition to managing sales budgets and expenses and undertaking secretarial duties for the sales and marketing team
- Coordinating exhibitions, conferences and seminars in addition to organising mailshots and sourcing promotional items, liaising effectively with a range of suppliers and agencies
- Producing sales and marketing presentations as well as maintaining the database and delivering training as required

EDUCATION AND QUALIFICATIONS

ECDL   European Computer Driving Licence

NVQ2   Customer Services
5 GCSEs   Including English and Mathematics

FURTHER SKILLS

IT proficiency   MS Office, MS Project and SPSS
Languages   Intermediate Spanish

OTHER DETAILS

Driving licence   Full/clean
Interests include   Hockey (captained Luton 2nd Eleven), yoga and violin

REFERENCES ARE AVAILABLE ON REQUEST

FIGURE 29.3

ANTONIA FARRER
1 Any Road, Anytown AN1 1CV
Telephone: 01632 960 739 (Home); 07700 900 709 (Mobile)
E-mail: antoniafarrer@example.com

Professional Profile

A dedicated and results-driven senior manager with a highly successful background in the achievement of profitable business growth through the creation and execution of successful sales and marketing strategies. Experienced in working with leading brands in the competitive retail and automotive industries with the primary focus on exceeding expectations for customer service delivery while ensuring optimum brand impact. Possesses excellent interpersonal, communication and negotiation skills and the ability to develop and maintain mutually beneficial internal and external relationships. Enjoys being part of, as well as managing, motivating and training, a successful and productive team, and thrives in highly pressurised and challenging working environments.

Career Summary

2005–2009   TYRES UK LTD
Freelance Consultant/Interim Network Development Manager

- Project managing the redevelopment of the retail sales strategy across the UK market with the ultimate aim of facilitating business performance improvements
- Successfully developing multi-channel solutions including instigating a new HiQ Fast Fit Franchise proposition
- Playing a pivotal role in the design and development of a class-leading B2C eBusiness website
- Working in close conjunction with external professionals to create and implement a retail network representation plan
- Actively involved in developing a new retail store concept and in redrafting all contractual agreements and process/procedure manuals
- Coordinating the pitch and scoping process for the selection of a staff training and development academy

1999–2005   BDW GROUP
2005–2005   Managing Director, BDW Contact Ltd

- Fully accountable for the establishment and management of a new business arm specialising in the provision of telemarketing services requiring the development of an independent customer base

Career Summary cont.

- Collaborating with professionals and third parties to set up the infrastructure for the company and coordinating the recruitment, selection and training of 15 members of staff
- Planning and organising a highly successful launch programme and driving the business forward to break-even three months ahead of projections
- Introducing a range of B2B and B2C services and facilitating the provision of 24-hour service by business partnership in conjunction with an external agency

2000–2004   Operations Director

- Providing management and support to up to 68 members of staff and motivating them towards the achievement of optimum service delivery standards to facilitate customer satisfaction and maximum revenue generation
- Maintaining full profit and loss accountability up to £5 million while achieving a year-on-year growth in revenue of more than 10%
- Initiating half-yearly service reviews with major blue-chip retail clients and formalising account planning to ensure best practice resulting directly in recognition for excellence in customer surveys
- Developing and implementing new billing and forecasting systems which significantly improved overall efficiency
- Enabling a 5% increase in actual gross margin in one year through the implementation of a staff incentive scheme

1999–2000   Account Director

- Working in close conjunction with key client representatives to develop marketing strategies and point-of-sale materials on behalf of retail partners
- Negotiating and securing £120,000 in bespoke systems development revenue and playing a key role in increasing monthly revenue from £12,000 to £100,000

1996–1999   WORDS PICTURES SOUNDS
Managing Director

- Setting up and developing a full service design agency from the initial business planning, financial forecasting and business strategy development through to building and retaining the customer base
- Successfully securing and effectively managing contracts with leading brands including Audi, One 2 One and Cadbury for the provision of a range of creative services including media creative, brochure design, corporate identity and hard point of sale
- Achieving approved supplier status with Audi and One 2 One and delivering sustained income growth with the turnover increasing from £75,000 in 1996 to £750,000 in 1999

Career Summary cont.

1983–1996   **VAG (UK) LTD**
                  Audi A8 Project Manager

- Commencing employment as a Trainee Field Sales Manager on behalf of the sole importers of Volkswagen and Audi vehicles and parts into the UK
- Gaining a series of promotions through various product, marketing, operations and advertising management positions, both head office and field based
- Ultimately undertaking the head office role of Audi A8 Project Manager tasked with the development and promotion of the brand and the vehicle within the luxury market with a total spend of £1.5 million

Education and Qualifications

4 A Levels   Mathematics, Economics, History and General Studies
8 O Levels   Including English and Mathematics

Professional Development

- Management Development Programme
- Marketing Management
- Presentation Skills
- Finance for Non-financial Managers
- Effective People Management
- Appraisal Training
- Team Building
- Creativity Training

IT Skills

- Word, Excel, Access, PowerPoint, Internet and e-mail

Personal Details

Driving Licence   Full/clean
Health   Excellent; non-smoker
Interests   Squash, golf, reading (current affairs), theatre and cuisine

References Are Available On Request

FIGURE 29.4

Jonathan Singh

address: 1 Any Road, Anytown AN1 1CV

telephone: 01632 960 939

mobile: 07700 900 232

e-mail: jonathansingh@example.com

Professional profile

A dynamic senior manager with extensive procurement operations and project management experience within the retail sector. A competent strategist capable of developing innovative plans and activities designed to facilitate competitive growth and competitive superiority. Possesses excellent interpersonal, communication and negotiation skills, the ability to influence decisions and to develop positive relationships both internally and externally. Enjoys being part of, as well as managing, motivating, training and developing, a successful and productive team and thrives in highly pressurised and challenging working environments.

Career summary

2004–date   J SAINSBURY PLC

2008–date   Senior Project Manager – International Buying Office

- Creating and implementing an innovative strategy to facilitate the seamless integration of Turkey and Asia into IBO procurement
- Additionally responsible for the development of a key strategy for the Global Direct Sourcing function

2008   Senior Buying Manager – Added Value Foods

- Fully accountable for the Beers, Ales and Cider category with £711 million sales delivered across the UK and ROI on brands and own brand products
- Providing management and support to a dedicated buying and marketing team and motivating them towards the achievement of objectives
- Successfully streamlining processes whilst creating a buying scale by leveraging the international business
- Proactively managing increasing challenges including rising costs of commodities, duty and energy to enable J Sainsbury to outperform the market and retain market share

Key Achievements

- Successfully overachieving budgeted sales by 12% (£25 million) whilst negotiating an additional £12 million in business plan support

Career summary cont.

2004–2008   **Head of Category – Produce Group Sourcing**

- Personally responsible for the creation and implementation of a Produce Central Buying Process to leverage economy of scale for J Sainsbury group and facilitate subsequent cost savings
- Managing day-to-day operations within group-sourced Fresh Produce category (vegetables, salads and horticulture) with responsibility for strategic growth and development
- Responsible for €208 million sales across the group with a team of Buyers and Buying Managers based in UK, Ireland, Slovakia, Czech Republic, Hungary and Poland
- Delivering increased product quality and reduced costs in accordance with customer expectations as a direct result of developing capability within the team and the supply base

Key Achievements

- Receiving an award from Sainsbury's main board for delivering group savings of £20 million in the first year whilst simultaneously overachieving the savings budget by £800,000
- Consolidating and establishing fresh hubs in Czech Republic, Slovakia, Poland and Hungary to leverage economy of scale
- Leading on the implementation of a new buying structure, involving substantial operational change, new processes and systems to enable a move towards a Group Procurement Strategy and the implementation of best practices
- Playing a pivotal role as a senior member of a leadership team tasked with creating and expanding a multinational produce buying team in the UK with achievements including delivering 60% of produce and horticulture procurement in CE and 5.5% of produce procurement in UK
- Introducing an innovative new range of cut flowers in CE with an annual budget of €20 million delivering 25% margin
- Establishing direct procurement from growers of Indian and Thai cut flowers to facilitate the delivery of the direct sourcing strategy

2003–2004   **UNITED WORLD COMMUNICATIONS, NAIROBI, KENYA**
                   Owner / Executive Director

- Establishing and managing a communications centre in Nairobi to provide unique communications options for the general and expatriate business community to enable NGOs and Missions to securely transact the financial aspects of their organisations

1997–2003   **TESCO UK LTD**
                   Head of Fresh Produce Procurement UK & ROI

- Commencing employment in a retail management and store expansion capacity before progressing through to Head of Produce responsible for seasonal non-food buying for UK and ROI

Career summary cont.

- Managing departmental operations covering 400 stores and 7 regional distribution centres with full accountability for 13% of company sales, £90 million annual turnover and profit margins in excess of 40%

Key Achievements

- Successfully doubling sales participation from 6.5% to 13% whilst driving a strong annual like for like of 15% and overall growth of 35% over three years
- Establishing a successful seven-days fresh cut flower business delivering 500% growth in the first year

1995–1996	**REGAL MOVING & STORAGE INC, NEW YORK, USA** Director
1992–1994	**REPAKS TRANSPORTE GESMBHH, VIENNA, AUSTRIA** Managing Director/Owner
1990–1992	**UN DISENGAGEMENT OBSERVER FORCES, DAMASCUS, SYRIA** Military Police

Formal qualifications

Leadership Development Programme (2009)

- Business Leaders of Today
- Create the Vision & the Need for Change
- Sell & Communicate with Impact
- Gain Commitment & Engage Team
- Business Plan

Professional training

- Negotiation Skills
- Ethical Buying
- Advanced Negotiation Skills
- Situational Leadership
- Range Management
- Competition Act
- Coaching & Feedback
- Performance Management

Other details

Languages	Fluent German
IT proficiency	Word, Excel, PowerPoint and GMIS
Driving licence	Full/clean
Interests include	Swimming, cycling, triathlons and art (painting)

References are available on request

Summary

- Your CV is your personal sales brochure and should be very carefully written and presented – to really showcase your talent.

- Your CV should be headed with your name – not 'Curriculum vitae' – boldly and clearly – before any other details – contact details, etc.

- Include a sufficiently detailed and very carefully phrased professional profile and objective at the beginning of the CV.

- It is a standard convention on CVs to use reverse chronological order, ie to present your most recent information first, followed by older information.

- Avoid superfluous details such as date of birth, marital status, nationality, number (and ages) of children/dependants, details of referees, etc.

- If you can include an achievements section then it can make an instant and dramatic difference to the power of your CV.

- If possible, tailor your CV according to the specific vacancy to which you are applying. A carefully targeted CV can easily mean the difference between success and failure.

- Spelling and grammatical errors are amongst the most irritating errors a recruiter sees – and also amongst the most easily avoided. The answer is to check, check and check again.

PART SEVEN
MY FIVE TOP TIPS TO SURVIVE AND THRIVE IN YOUR NEW JOB

30
Survive and thrive

If you only had time to read one chapter of *Ultimate New Job*, this is the chapter I would most like you to have taken the time to read. See it as a 'cheat sheet'. It encapsulates some of the most important principles that we have covered in the book. Make an effort to accommodate all these when starting your new job and you'll immediately be well above average.

1. Whether you feel confident or not, make sure you look it

You might feel like you're back to your first day at school – a little lost. But be aware that confident people inspire confidence in others – if you appear confident that you are able to do the job, everyone around you is likely to be more inclined to believe that you can. It's human nature.

2. Make an outstanding first impression

Make a poor first impression and you might not be able to recover from it. How quickly do you sum up someone you've just met? It's probably just a couple of minutes. Make sure that you make a powerful first impression on everyone you meet – start your new relationships off on a positive foot. Start as you mean to go on.

3. Build successful relationships

The only real way to build relationships is to take the time and to make the effort to get to know people. First off, you need to ask for and then remember people's names. You then need to find out more about them; start building up a mental file on them. The little things count too, like saying, 'Good morning!' and asking how people are. It's surprising how important these little everyday interactions can be. Don't neglect them.

4. Watch what comes out of your mouth!

Think before you speak. Steer clear of saying anything too personal or anything which could be remotely controversial or which could potentially cause any offence to anyone. Tact is the word. Stick to small talk. It can be all too easy to say something which you might later come to regret. Remember: EBBOM… engage brain before opening mouth!

5. Fill gaps in your knowledge

It's entirely understandable that there will be gaps in your knowledge and that you won't know how to do certain things. The best way to overcome this is to ask questions. You will avoid needless mistakes. It's a good idea to keep a notebook with you and take notes as you are shown new aspects of your job. This should help ensure that you don't have to repeatedly ask the same questions and will help you to keep firmly on top of things.

Conclusion

Successfully starting a new job is not rocket science! Most of what I have outlined is reasonably simple to take on board and it's just a matter of putting in the necessary time and effort.

I do hope you have found *Ultimate New Job* useful. Don't forget to visit The CV Centre's online forum to let us know how you get on: **www.ineedacv.co.uk/forum**.

You will also have the opportunity to make contact with me and my team directly. GOOD LUCK!

APPENDIX

THE 15 MOST COMMON MISTAKES – AND HOW TO AVOID THEM!

The same common mistakes crop up time and time again when people start new jobs. Too many people fail to achieve their full potential because of a small number of easily avoided blunders.

Some of the mistakes that people make when starting a new job are very obvious and others are more subtle. The CV Centre has conducted a comprehensive survey to derive a 'Top 15' and, in this appendix, I will list these 15 most common mistakes and refer you back to previous sections of this book, to explain both why they are a mistake and how to avoid them.

1. Not understanding the job

Preparation is everything. And the key to preventing any new job jitters is to prepare yourself thoroughly.

We fear what we don't know and what we can't control, yet there is so much you can do to plan and prepare for your new job. Success in a new job, particularly at more senior levels of management, is often built on the thinking you undertake and the focus you develop before you even take up the post.

In most cases, you will have a notice period to serve out with your current employer and you can use this time to prepare – the better prepared you are, the fewer your reasons to be nervous.

The first item on your list should be to thoroughly understand the job in question.

For further guidance on researching and understanding your job, please refer back to Chapter 3, Being prepared.

2. Making a poor first impression

First impressions count. Before you get close to doing any actual work, the first thing you'll be doing is 'meeting and greeting' – and first impressions are extremely important. Everyone you meet in your first few days will be making initial judgements about you – and often on the basis of just a few minutes spent together. Sounds scary? It's not really. It's what you do naturally every day when you meet new people – when you go to a party, for example, or out for dinner with friends of friends. So don't put yourself under too much pressure. But do be conscious of the impression you'll be making on others.

Make a poor first impression and you might not be able to recover from it. How quickly do you sum up someone you've just met? It's probably just a couple of minutes. Make sure that you make a powerful first impression on everyone you meet today – start your new relationships off on a positive foot. Start as you mean to go on.

For further details on making an outstanding first impression, please refer back to Chapter 4, D-Day – your first day.

3. Putting your foot in it

Whilst it's obviously very important to come across as open and friendly with the people you meet, do keep your guard up. You don't know anything about these people; you don't know their backgrounds, their opinions, their characters; you don't know their relationships with each other. So watch what comes out of your mouth! Think before you speak. Steer clear of saying anything too personal or anything which could be remotely controversial or which could potentially cause any offence to anyone. Tact is the word. Stick to small talk. It can be all too easy to say something which you might later come to regret. Remember: EBBOM… Engage brain before opening mouth!

For more advice on how not to put your foot in it, please see Chapter 4, D-Day – your first day.

4. Failing to correctly manage your new boss

Quite simply, no other relationship is more important than your relationship with your new boss. Statistically, having problems with their boss is the number-one reason people give for changing jobs! Clearly, this is a relationship you need to get right – and right from the start.

When we think of managing, we normally think about managing our subordinates but there are various ways in which it is important that you should be managing your boss.

More on this in Chapter 7, Managing your new boss.

5. Incorrectly handling your subordinates

Albert Einstein said, 'I never teach my pupils; I only attempt to provide the conditions in which they can learn.' Successful people management is a lot like successful teaching – you need to inspire and motivate. That's what really counts. That's your job. Good leaders follow specific plans and put their subordinates first.

The most successful managers and executives achieve their objectives by aligning the aims of their employees with those of their organisation. Once an employee is able to under-stand – and empathise with – the overall aims of the organisation, they are normally much more motivated to help achieve them. Having ensured that the organisation and your subordinates are working towards the same objectives, you can then focus on exactly which motivational techniques can be implemented to facilitate the achievement of these goals. A well-motivated workforce is a more productive workforce. It is also one which tends to experience lower stress levels, lower absenteeism and increased job satisfaction and self-confidence.

For more on this issue, please refer back to Chapter 9, Handling your subordinates.

6. Not planning and organising yourself

Before you can set about planning and organising your workload, you need to be clear about what it is that you are planning and organising. Your first step is therefore to establish pre-cisely what your various goals are – and what their respective priorities are.

For many people, the single most important tool in planning and organisation is a comprehensive list and/or schedule of what work actually needs to be done, generally called a 'To Do' list.

You should always have a To Do list – and maybe even several.

I talk about this subject in greater detail back in Chapter 11, Planning and organisation.

7. Failing to manage your time properly

Arguably the most successful achievers across all industry sectors and professions are those who have learnt to manage their time effectively. If you can more effectively manage your daily workload, you will be able to increase your productivity whilst also ensuring you are able to maintain a healthy work–life balance.

Time management is not necessarily a fixed series of systems and procedures which apply to everyone – indeed, certain techniques that some people rely on simply do not suit other people. The key is to find a system that works for you and to stick to it.

To achieve successful time management you will need to put into place certain procedures but, most important, effective time management is a frame of mind. Be conscious of your level of productivity and, if you see time being lost or wasted then take steps to correct that. You should soon find that you are much more productive than before and that you waste far less time on trivial, unimportant and unnecessary tasks.

The issue of time management is covered in detail in Chapter 12, Time management.

8. Not delegating when necessary

If you have people to whom you can reliably delegate a task – and within whose job function it is to carry out such a task – then delegate it! So much time is lost by handling tasks which would be best delegated to someone else.

The perfectionists amongst us often have considerable difficulty with delegation. Perfectionists tend to fear that a task, once delegated, simply won't be carried out to an appropriately high standard. This may be true – but does it actually matter? Whilst perfection is always highly desirable, it's often not very practical. Does the task have to be carried out perfectly? (And who defines perfection, anyway?) Or does it just have to be carried out sufficiently well that it doesn't lead to any problems? When juggling a heavy workload, you have to know when to say no to perfection and accept a compromise. There just aren't enough hours in the day – or days in the week!

Whilst I'm not for one minute saying you're the sort of person who can't delegate, if you're looking for advice on this topic then take a look at Chapter 12, Time management.

9. Poor body language

Many experts agree that much of what we communicate when we communicate verbally isn't actually verbal; it's physical. Only a small minority of what we communicate is communicated by the actual words we say. Much more is communicated by the volume, pitch and rhythm of our voice and even more via our body language, in particular our facial expressions.

Everyone is inherently sensitive to certain nuances of body language. It's instinctive and its importance should not be underestimated.

What's all this about body language? Take a look at Chapter 13, Communication.

10. Communicating poorly

Establishing and maintaining effective channels of communication with your boss, with your colleagues and with anyone else you may work with – customers, suppliers, etc – are imperative.

Successful communication is all about building relationships, avoiding misunderstandings and enhancing productivity through the clear exchange of ideas. It clarifies thoughts, promotes understanding and leads to action.

And it is worth noting that communication involves both speaking and listening so that mutual understanding is achieved.

I talk more about the basic principles of communication in Chapter 13, Communication.

11. Letting difficult people get you down

How you handle difficult people will demonstrate pretty much everything anyone needs to know about your interpersonal skills.

When it comes to dealing with interpersonal conflict, there are three main ways in which you might react:

- Do you clash head-on with difficult people?

- Do you run away and hide?!

- Do you find ways to deal with them?

Which of these three categories do you fall into?

More about this in Chapter 19, Dealing with difficult people.

12. Engaging in office politics and gossip

Is it our qualifications that help us to move up the career ladder? Is it our experience? No, it's other people! Whether we like it or not, the people we work with have a much greater influence on how far our careers progress than do our actual talents or work ethic.

Many people think their workplaces are devoid of office politics; they're generally not. And it's normally those who are the most politically savvy who manage to make their way to the top fastest.

That doesn't mean you need to indulge in office politics, though.

This important topic is discussed in greater detail in Chapter 20, Handling office politics.

13. Failing to cope with pressure and stress

The ability to cope with pressure and stress is essential in almost all walks of life, whether you're working checkout at the supermarket or heading up a major corporation. Pressure and stress are unavoidable aspects of the world we live in.

In recent times, stress has increasingly become one of the most common causes of absence from work, often leading to long-term absence or even resignation. Many employers are becoming aware of the importance of the well-being of their staff to maintaining productivity levels and are therefore introducing specific policies to ensure the effective management of stress in the workplace.

There are a number of factors recognised as being triggers of stress and stress-related illnesses and these can be found both at home and in the workplace. The symptoms vary dramatically from person to person and can be relatively minor or, at the other end of the spectrum, can be very severely debilitating. The key is stress prevention and there are many effective techniques that both an individual and their employer can use to prevent, reduce and manage stress within the workplace.

If you're suffering from stress or prone to doing so then please take the time to read through Chapter 21, Pressure and stress.

14. Forgetting about ongoing training

If you want to progress then it's important to take a proactive approach to your own career development.

Training might be an issue you specifically covered when negotiating your original package with your new employer and you may well have a formal training allowance allocated to you.

Whether there is or isn't a formal training structure in place with your new employer, you should go out of your way to take part in any available training, workshops or seminars that may help you to develop your skills and knowledge, and also seek to obtain support from your employer for any external training or professional qualifications.

Your employer, if they have any sense, should be keen to see you taking an active interest in the development of your career as it should mean that you are ultimately able to make a more positive contribution to the overall improvement of the organisation.

For a longer discussion on this topic please refer back to Chapter 25, Training.

15. Not being prepared for performance appraisals

Not all organisations operate a formal system of performance appraisals but most organisations will appraise your performance in one way or another at certain intervals. There are many different types of performance appraisal, ranging from a quick chat with the boss over a cup of tea to a more rigid – and documented – appraisal, typical of larger organisations.

The thought of a forthcoming performance appraisal can be enough to send shivers down the spine of even the most hardened professional. It's a lot like a job interview – and it's natural to be a little apprehensive. Appraisals can be seen as an opportunity for your manager to voice their gripes and dissatisfaction and to generally criticise. However, the true and proper aim of a performance appraisal is to motivate and develop an employee and, if approached correctly by you and your manager, there is no reason why the whole experience cannot be both rewarding and positive. A good manager should try to make your appraisal reasonably informal and non-confrontational.

As always, preparation is key – and performance appraisals are covered in Chapter 26, Performance appraisals.

16. Not enjoying yourself!

Yes, I know I said this appendix would cover the 15 most common mistakes – but everyone loves a bonus, don't they?!

So here's a 16th mistake for you: Not enjoying yourself.

Who was it that said, 'If work was fun we'd call it play'? Well, whoever it was, they were wrong. We all spend a very significant proportion of our short lives on this planet 'stuck' at work – so you may as well enjoy it! Make an effort to enjoy your work and it's much more likely that you will in fact enjoy it – and that others will find you a more enjoyable person in whose company to be. Life's too short not to enjoy your work!

FURTHER READING AND RESOURCES

Recommended books

Innes, J (2009) *Brilliant Cover Letters*, Prentice Hall Business, Harlow

Innes, J (2009) *The CV Book*, Prentice Hall Business, Harlow

Innes, J (2009) *The Interview Book*, Prentice Hall Business, Harlow

Innes, J (2012) *The Interview Question & Answer Book*, Prentice Hall Business, Harlow

Karseras, H (2006) *From New Recruit to High Flyer*, Kogan Page, London

Kay, F (2006) *New Kid on the Block*, Marshall Cavendish Business, Singapore

Kay, F (2010) *Successful Networking*, Kogan Page, London

Liebling, M (2009) *How People Tick*, 2nd edn, Kogan Page, London

Liebling, M (2009) *Working with the Enemy*, Kogan Page, London

Lilley, R (2010) *Dealing with Difficult People*, Kogan Page, London

Phillips, T (2011) *Talk Normal*, Kogan Page, London

Taylor, R (2011) *Confidence at Work*, Kogan Page, London

These titles are available from all major bookshops. You can also learn more about them and even place an order for a copy by visiting the following page on our website: **www.ineedacv.co.uk/recommendedbooks4**.

Online resources

I keep my list of online resources... online. That way I can keep it bang up to date at all times. Please access the following page for a wide range of useful links to job sites and other online resources: **www.ineedacv.co.uk/resources**.

INDEX

Page numbers in *italic* indicate figures

15 common mistakes – and avoiding them
197–203
communicating poorly   201
engaging in office politics and gossip
201
failing to cope with pressure and stress
202
failing to manage your new boss correctly
198–99
failing to manage your time properly
199–200
forgetting about ongoing training   202
handling your subordinates incorrectly
199
lack of preparedness for performance
appraisals   202–03
letting difficult people get you down   201
making poor first impression   198
not delegating when necessary   200
not enjoying yourself   203
not planning and organising
yourself   199
not understanding the job   197–98
poor body language   200
putting your foot in it   198
15 questions asked when starting a new job
xx–xxi

activity log   78–79 *see also* to-do lists
assertiveness   120–26
defining   120, 126
questions to check your own   124–25
tips for developing/practising   123–24

being prepared   *see* preparation for
new job

body language   81–83 *see also* smiling
copying   83, 86
eye contact   73, 86, 96
negative   82
poor   200
reading others'   82
tone of voice   83, 86
breathing deeply/slowly   30, 95
briefing   22–23
brinkmanship, avoiding   6
bullies/bullying   121–22, 126, 133
see also assertiveness

change at work   139–43 *see also* imposing
change at work
coping with   141–42, 143
impact of   140
and importance of communication   140
and neuro-linguistic programming (NLP)
141
reasons for   139–40, 142
seizing opportunities of   140–41, 143
stress caused by   142
and training   141, 143
understanding your role   142
chapter summaries   14, 20, 24, 34, 38, 42,
49–50, 54, 60, 64–65, 72–73, 80,
86, 92–93, 97, 101–02, 108,
114–15, 125–26, 130, 137–38,
142–43, 148, 152, 157–58, 163, 168,
174, 191, 196
communication   81–86, 140 *see also* body
language
by e-mail   84–85
poor   201
within organisation, lack of   145

by telephone   83–84
by videoconferencing and webcams   84
confidence (in)   **6, 23,** 34, 83, 104, 166
   inspiring   195
   lack of   82
   losing   144
   over-   28, 82
   self-   56, 58, 60, 120–22, 199
conflict   see dealing with difficult people
curriculum vitae (CVs)   175–91
   avoiding mistakes in writing   176–79
      see also CV writing mistakes
   laying foundations: getting the basics
      right   175–76, 191
   templates for   179–80, *180–81, 182–84,*
     185–87, 188–90
   tips to make your CV stand out   179, 191
   website for free templates   180
CV Centre website   xvii–xviii, 196
CV writing mistakes   176–79
   date of birth included   178
   excessive details of interests   178
   inappropriate heading   176
   inappropriate section order   177
   inclusion of photographs   176
   lack of clear section headings/separation
     of sections   177
   lack of proper professional profile and/or
     objective   177
   length   179
   missing/inappropriate e-mail addresses
     176
   no bullet pointing   178
   referees included   178
   reverse chronological order not used
     178, 191
   spelling, grammar and typos   178, 191
   superfluous personal details   177, 191
   writing in the first person   177
D-Day   see your first day in your new job
dealing with difficult people (and)   119–26
   assertiveness   120–21, 123–24, 126
     see also main entry
   being nice to bullies   122
   coping with bullies   121–22, 126
     see also bullies/bullying
   differences between team players and
     bullies   121

empathy   126
   by keeping calm/believing in yourself
     122
   questionnaire on your assertiveness
     124–25
   sexual harassment   122–23
Dick, P.K.   129

EBBOM (engage brain before opening
     mouth)   31, 196, 198
e-mail   16, 40, 78–80, 84–85, 86, 107
   address   72, 73
   on CVs   176
   content   85
   etiquette   85
   practicalities for   85
emotional intelligence   62, 65
empathy   56, 62, 64, 120, 126, 199

finding your place in the team (by)   51–54
   becoming a better team player   52–53
     key tips for   53
   demonstrating trust and respect   53–54
   developing team relationships   51–52
   keeping confidences   53–54
   understanding hierarchy   52
first impressions   28–29, 34, 195, 198

handling your subordinates (by/with)
     55–60
   delegation   59
   determining their motivations   57, 60
   motivational posters   59, 60
   motivational techniques for   56–57, 60
   rewards and incentives   58, 60
   setting targets   58, 60
   team-building exercises   58–59, 60
   ten top tips for   55
   training and coaching   58

imposing change at work   144–48
   and change for the sake of it   147, 148
   effects of   144–45
   and managing organisational change (by)
     146–47, 148
     discussing what is involved   146
     explaining need for change   146
     implementing change   147

providing training and support   147
reinforcing change   147
and statutory obligations of organisation/
    rights of workforce   146
successful implementation of   145–46

job offers (and)   3–14
bargaining strategies   5–6
consideration of   8
details of package   3–4
maintaining confidence   6
multiple and counter-   8
negotiating salary   5, 14
reaching agreement   6
references and referees   10–11, *11, 12,*
    13, 14
rejection letters   18–19, *19,* 20
researching the package   4
salary negotiation   4–5, 6–7, *7–8*
worst-case scenario   6–7
written acceptance of   8–9, *9,* 14
written statement of employment   9
jumping ship *see* leaving your new job

knowledge, developing your (by/of)
    39–42
continuous learning   41
corporate language   40, 42
note-taking   39, 42
people you may never meet   41, 42
skeletons in the cupboard   41, 42
understanding protocol   40
knowledge, filling gaps in your   32, 39, 196

leaving your last job (and)   15–20
counter-offers   18, 20
exit interviews   18
letter/e-mail of resignation   16, *17,* 20
notice periods for   15, 16
reasons for   15
rejection letters , 18–19, *19*
summary   20
leaving your new job (and) 149–52
assessing reasons for   149, 152
final consideration of reasons for
    151–52
implications for future recruitment   151,
    152

possible changes in your role   150–51,
    152
questionnaire to gauge your
    unhappiness   150
legislation
    Employment Act (2002)   135
    Employment Equality (Age) Regulations
        (2008)   178
LinkedIn   63–65

managing your new boss (by)   45–50
assisting in decision-making   45–46, 49
discussion and conversation   48–49, 50
expressing your ideas/opinions   47–48,
    50
finding solutions for problems   46–47,
    49
golden rules for   49
keeping them informed   48
'managing upward'   47
and your working relationship   49, 50
meetings   98–102
controlling   100–101, 102
establishing purpose of   98, 101
follow-up of   101, 102
opening   100
preparing venue for   99–100, 102
selecting date, time and venue
    of   98–99, 102
setting agenda for   99, 102
moving on   *see* curriculum vitae (CV)

networking and socialising   61–65
online   63, 65 *see also* LinkedIn
in person through off-the-job
    training   62–63, 65
by rapport with people   62, 65
ten top tips for   63–64
and using your network   64, 65
neuro-linguistic programming (NLP)   141

office politics (and)   127–30
achieving win–win situations   128–29,
    130
dirty tricks   128, 130
gossip   129–30
reality of   127–28
online forum (CV Centre)   xx, 196

pay rises (and)   164–68
  avoiding threats   167, 168
  discussing with your employer   166
  proving your value   166, 168
  requesting   164
  sample request letter   *167–68*
  tact and diplomacy   165–66, 168
  timing of request for   164–65, 168
perfection, saying no to   76
performance appraisals (and)   159–63
  aim of   159
  dealing with negative issues   161
  preparation for   159, 163
  questions for advance consideration
      161–63
  targets/objectives as future
      benchmarks   160, 163
  win–win situation   161
Peter, L J   47
  and managing upward   47
The Peter Principle   47
planning and organisation (and)   xvi, 69–73
  achieving your goals   72
  acquiring e-mail address   72, 73
  distinguishing between important and
      urgent tasks   70–71, 72
  maintaining your focus   71
  priorities for   70
  'to do' list   69–70, 71, 72–73
  of your tools and work
      environment   71–72, 73
PowerPoint   96
preparation for new job (by)   21–24
  learning from past experience   24
  researching the organisation   22
  researching the organisation's
      environment   22
  understanding the job   21–22
  understanding your reasons for change
      23
  using your research   23
presentations (and)   94–97
  clear and logical structure of   94, 97
  cue cards   96, 97
  eye contact   96, 97
  guidelines for   94, 97
  nerve-calming tips   94–95, 97

physical gestures   96
PowerPoint   96
preparing and practising for   94, 97
questions from the audience   97
using visualisation   95
visual aids   96
pressure and stress   131–38 *see also*
      stress
  causes of   132–3
  difference between   131
  failure to cope with   202
  work–life balance   135–37, 138
  work–life balance questionnaire
      136–37
  in the workplace   131–32
promotion   169–74
  interview   173
  opportunities for   169
  and pay rise   173
  reasons why you deserve   171, *172*, 174
  speculative approach to   170
  ten tips for winning   170–71

reading and resources   204
recruitment consultancies   4, 6
relationships, building   29–30, 51–52,
      196
remote working/working from home
      103–08 *see also* working abroad
  advantages of   104
  and business travel   106–07
  and importance of regular breaks   106
  overcoming difficulties of   105–06
  successful   104
  tips for   105
research on
  communication   81
  multi-tasking   78, 80
respect   49, 53–54, 62, 141, 150, 166
      see also trust
  mutual   52

smiling   30, 33, 34, 84, 95
stress   131–38, 142
  causes of   132–33, 137
      and negative factors   132–33
  combating   134, 137

effects of   133–34, 137
   and common mental symptoms   133
  failure to cope with   202
  identifying triggers of   138
  as serious illness   134, 138
subordinates   *see* handling your
    subordinates
survive and thrive (through)   195–96
  building successful relationships   196
  confidence   195
  filling gaps in your knowledge   196
  first impressions   195
  tact   196

teams *see also* finding your place in the
    team
  and team-building exercises   58–59, 60
teamwork   54
time management (and)   74–80
  activity logs   78
  categorising e-mail   79, 80
  de-cluttering   79, 80
  delegation   76–77, 80
  interruptions and the unexpected   77
  multi-tasking   78, 80
  procrastination   74–75, 80
  refusing tasks   75–76
  relaxation   79–80
to-do lists   69–70, 71, 72–73, 75, 77–78,
    199
top tips for
  asking for a pay rise   165
  confident speaking   95
  copying others' body language   83
  dealing with gossip   129–30
  developing effective working relationship
    with your boss   46
  differences/similarities in working cultures
    40
  exit interviews/leaving employment   18
  first day in your new job   28
  first impressions   29
  handling job offers   6
  identifying and emulating successful
    colleagues   52
  nervousness   30
  noting information on your first day   32

presentations   84
seeking promotion   170
translating personal titles abroad,
    eg Mrs – Mme   110
understanding your new job   24
training   58, 141, 143, 155–58
  forgetting ongoing   202
  identifying possibilities for   155–56, 157
  off-the-job   62–63, 65
  and professional memberships   157,
    158
  and professional qualifications   156–57,
    158
trust   53–54, 62, 77, 83, 106, 144, 146

understanding your purpose (and)   35–38
  job description *vis à vis* day-to-day reality
    36, 38
  relative to overall organisational aims/
    objectives   37, 38
  researching organisational
    environment   37, 38

visualisation   95

website: http://www.linkedin.com/in/
    jamesinnes   63
working abroad (in)   107, 109–15
  Australia and New Zealand   113, 115
  Canada   112–13, 115
  European Economic Area (EEA) 107
  France and Belgium   109–10
    and French culture/language   110
  Germany, Austria, Switzerland   110–11,
    114
  and health care/insurance   107, 108
  learning new languages   107, 108
  Ireland (Éire)   109, 114
  Italy   111, 114
  The Middle East   113, 115
    and economic 'free zones'   113
  and personal titles, eg. Mrs – Mme   110,
    114
  South Africa   113
  South America   114
    medical/psychological examinations in
    114

Spain   111–12, 114
United States of America   112, 115
usefulness of guide books   107
writing skills (and)   87–93
American usage   89–90, 93
apostrophes   92
commonly misspelled words   87–88
double-checking your document   87, 93
easily confused words   88–89
fully capitalised words   90, 93
punctuation   92
setting default language in Microsoft Word
   90, 93
slips of the tongue   91
typos   91

Young, E   74
your first day in your new job (and)   27–34
after work   33, 34
building working relationships   29–30
feeling nervous and anxious   30, 32, 34
first impressions for   28–29, 34, 195
looking confident for   28
lunchtime   31–32
and sociability   31
organising your workspace/note-taking
   32–33
tact and mindfulness   31, 34
setting off for   27
tea-time   33
value of a smile   30, 33, 34